handy homework helper

How to Write School Reports

Writer:
Helen H. Moore

Consultant:
Carl B. Smith, Ph.D.

Publications International, Ltd.

Louis Weber, C.E.O.
Publications International, Ltd.
7373 North Cicero Avenue
Lincolnwood, Illinois 60712

Permission is never granted for commercial purposes.

Manufactured in China.

8 7 6 5 4 3 2 1

ISBN: 0-7853-3490-4

Helen H. Moore is a journalist, poet, and published author of educational and children's books. She has taught language arts for elementary school grades and served as an editor for a national educational publisher. Her work includes *A Poem a Day: 180 Thematic Poems and Activities That Teach and Delight All Year Long* and *The 100 Best Brain-Boosters: Puzzles and Games to Stimulate Students' Thinking.*

Carl B. Smith, Ph.D., is Professor Emeritus at Indiana University and directs the Education Resource Information Center (ERIC) for reading, English and communication, and the Family Literacy Center. In 1997 Dr. Smith received the Indiana Literacy Award for his many contributions to reading instruction across the country. He has authored over 40 books for teachers and parents including *Help Your Child Read and Succeed* and *Improving Your Children's Composition.*

Illustrations: Chris Reed

Contents

About This Book

There's no getting away from it: Every student needs to learn how to write and present written and oral reports. Although it might seem scary, it's actually an important task. Reports are helpful tools for both students and teachers.

For you, the student, preparing reports is a great way to increase your own in-depth knowledge of a subject, making you an "expert" in the field you've chosen to write about. Preparing reports also helps sharpen your powers of observation and your thinking and decision-making skills. In addition, the process of preparing and presenting a report exercises your mind as you brainstorm a topic, research information, put it into a final form for presentation, and present it to your teacher or classmates.

Reports are an important tool for your teachers, too. Reading or listening to your report gives teachers a very clear picture of just what your strengths are as a student. Reports can even let teachers know where you might need some additional help. This is especially important if you're one of those students who knows your subject, but "freezes up" on tests or finds it hard to participate in class discussions. Reports give your teacher more opportunities to see you shine.

This book is a guide to writing and presenting great written and oral reports. In it you'll learn just what teachers look for in a good report. You'll learn different ways to select topics, where to find information, how to take and organize notes, how to transform your notes into a well-written report, and more. You'll find handy charts and checklists to help you through every step of the process, from selecting your topic to handing in your finished draft or making a classroom speech.

Read through this book once without trying to memorize it. Then when you get your next report assignment, refer to this book each step of the way. You don't have to follow each one of the book's suggestions exactly; you can adapt them to your own learning style. Every chapter will give you enough guidance so that you'll soon be on your way to becoming an "Ace Report-er."

Me? Write a Report?

You might be surprised to discover that you are already a reporter in some ways. Most of us have had an experience like this: You run indoors to tell your mom that your brother or sister is doing something he or she shouldn't be doing. Chances are, after your mom is able to get you calmed down, the conversation goes something like this:

> **Mom:** "Stop fussing, and tell me exactly what happened."
>
> **You:** "Well, first I was riding my bike, and then Allie came along and said, 'I want to ride,' and then I said, 'No, it's my bike,' and then she said, 'too bad,' and grabbed the handlebars, and that's when I came in here to find you."
>
> **Mom:** "Well, we'll just see about that!"

That kind of report had an attention-getting opening, a middle, and an end. The events were arranged in the order in which they happened. And even though Mom wasn't present, after hearing your report of the incident she had a good idea of what took place, thanks to your clear reporting. The report was pretty persuasive, too—it inspired Mom to take immediate action! That's one of the basic ideas behind reports. If you get the readers' attention, inform them, persuade them, entertain them, or convince them of your point of view, you've done a great job!

What's a Report? Why Write Them?

Think of the articles you read in the local newspaper or the stories you watch on the nightly news. The reporters make it possible for you, the reader or viewer, to know all about events that you couldn't possibly have witnessed or experienced yourself. Yet due to the reporters' thorough research and skillful presentation, you are able to learn about occurrences that may have taken place half a block or half a world away, increasing your store of knowledge and enriching your life.

Of course, the reports you prepare for school are a little different from the kinds of reporting described here so far. But there are some similarities. The main similarity is that a good report provides enough information about a topic, and is organized well enough, so that a reader or listener feels he or she has a good understanding of that topic, even though that reader or listener did not do the research or experience the events being reported.

What Makes a Good Report?

A good report is organized; it has an introduction, a body, and a conclusion. A written report is organized into paragraphs. An oral report is also organized into paragraphs so listeners can follow along without confusion, although the listeners might not be able to tell where each new paragraph starts.

The introductory paragraph, obviously, must tell what the report is about. But it should also grab the reader's attention. You

---

Simile: a comparison using the words "like" or "as." "Her smile was wide and bright as the summer sky at noon." "The dancer's tap shoes hitting the stage sounded like firecrackers on the Fourth of July."

Metaphor: a stronger comparison that does not use the words "like" or "as"; instead, it says that one thing *is* another thing. "His terrified heart was a caged bird, beating its wings against the bars of its cage." "The engineer's arm is a piston, pumping furiously as he loads the coal."

can be sure your introductory paragraph is appealing by using interesting and descriptive vocabulary as well as metaphors and similes.

The body of the report is also written in paragraphs. Each paragraph must be about only one topic, have an introductory or topic sentence, contain supporting details, and contain only sentences that are necessary and related to the topic. (And the sentences it contains must be complete and easy to understand.) In addition, the sentences of each paragraph must be arranged in an order that makes sense.

Just as the sentences within each paragraph must be arranged in an order that makes good sense, the paragraphs themselves must be arranged in an order so the whole report makes sense to a reader. The paragraphs can't jump around from one topic to the next haphazardly; this would confuse the reader. (Remember, the same rules apply for oral reports, which should be written down before they are presented orally. For more about oral reports, see Chapter 12.)

Elements of a Good Report

Introduction
includes a topic sentence that tells what the report is about

Body
several paragraphs that support the topic sentence

Conclusion
summarizes the report and lets the reader or listener know it's at an end

The concluding paragraph of a report must summarize the main points made in the report and also let the reader know that the report is at an end. In addition, every word you use must be spelled correctly throughout your report, and standard punctuation and capitalization are crucial.

If it all sounds a little overwhelming, don't worry. This book reviews many techniques and tools to help you create first-rate reports that contain all the elements discussed here. One of the most important techniques is one you may already know about. It's called "the writing process."

The Writing Process

The writing process is similar for both creative writing and report writing. One or two stages may be slightly different, but the beauty of the writing process is that it's not a rigid pattern. It's a flexible guideline that each writer can adapt to his or her own needs. Whether you are writing essays, stories, or reports, the writing process consists of several general stages.

The first stage is prewriting, which is the process of generating ideas, becoming inspired, conducting interviews, doing research, brainstorming, taking notes—just about everything that happens before you first put your pen to paper (or finger to keyboard) to create the first sentence of the first draft of your report. (Actually, a lot of writing does happen in the prewriting stage, but it's mostly in the

The Writing Process

Prewriting
brainstorming a topic, taking notes, doing research, making an outline

Drafting
putting ideas on paper and turning notes into sentences without focusing on spelling and grammar

Revising
improving what you've written based on your own evaluation and input from others

Proofreading
checking your writing for errors in spelling, punctuation, capitalization, and grammar

Publishing
sharing your writing with an audience, either in final written form (with no errors), in an oral presentation (speech), or in another alternative format

form of taking and organizing notes, not writing your report in its finished form.)

After prewriting comes the outline, rough draft, or drafting stage. This is the stage when you first try out your ideas, writing them down without being too concerned about spelling, punctuation, and grammar. You are just getting your thoughts out and organizing them on paper.

The next step is the revising stage. This is where you try to improve on your first draft. Based on your own evaluation or the opinion of a classmate, friend, parent, or teacher, you may decide to rearrange information, add or take out information, or replace some sentences and words.

Proofreading comes next. This is where you "worry" about all the things you didn't have to worry about in the rough draft stage. Now you check your writing for errors in spelling, punctuation, capitalization, and grammar before going on to make your final copy.

Publishing is the final stage. This is the big time! In this stage, you share your writing with an audience. A written report is only one way to "publish" your writing. Making speeches (or oral reports) and creating presentations with visual aids such as mobiles, posters, and slide shows are some others. (For more information on alternatives to traditional written or oral reports, see Chapter 11.)

The Stages of Report Writing

Writing a report is not very different from writing a short story, essay, or other creative piece. The main difference occurs in the prewriting stage, and it involves research.

When you write a creative piece, you likely generate your ideas out of your own feelings and experiences. In report writing, although the idea for the topic may come from your own feelings and inter-

HANDY TIP:

This book contains several checklists that can help you complete
the various stages of your reports. You might want to photocopy these
checklists and keep them near your work station, on your bulletin board, or
in a special section of your notebook so you can refer to them easily
and quickly when you are writing your next report.

ests, the finished report depends on facts and figures that you must
research before organizing and drafting your report. (Doing research is the subject of Chapter 3.)

Research can be fun and easy. Coming up with an idea to write
about and turning that idea into a report can be challenging. But
don't worry. The next chapter of this book suggests ways for you to
generate ideas for report topics; you'll be creating super reports in
no time.

Elements of Report Writing

The following activities are involved in creating an effective written or
oral report. You might not follow these steps in this order, and you
might not follow all of them, but this checklist includes all of the
activities covered in this book.

❑ Brainstorming ideas
❑ Selecting a topic
❑ Collecting details
❑ Doing research (using sources like books, newspapers, movies, Web
  sites, or interviews with people who know your topic)
❑ Taking notes
❑ Writing an outline
❑ Writing a rough draft
❑ Editing, proofreading, and/or revising your rough draft
❑ Publishing your written report or presenting your oral report

Generating Ideas

Now comes the fun part: deciding on your topic. In some cases, your teacher may assign a topic for you. But many teachers feel that students learn more and write better when writing about a subject they've chosen themselves. If this is the case with your assignment, then you're in luck! Look around you for ideas; the possibilities are endless.

Ideas for writing can come from your everyday life and surroundings. The people you live with, the people you meet, the hobbies and sports you pursue—any one of these things can be the basis for your writing. The entire writing process will become so much more interesting, valuable, and fun when you choose a topic that is of real interest to you. It's important, then, to learn how to choose your topics with care.

Where Do Ideas for Topics Come From?

Do you keep a journal? Personal journals can be a great source of ideas for writing topics. Look through your journal and see if any one topic appears more frequently than others. Whatever jumps out at you in this way will probably be something that interests you a great deal, that you've done a lot of thinking about, and that you feel strongly about.

A topic doesn't have to make you happy to interest you; in fact, you may find you have a lot to say about a topic that you have negative feelings about. Great writers have created masterpieces that protest injustice, expose a crime, or attempt to right a wrong. You may be surprised at what you can do with a topic that you dislike, or one that angers you.

Look at books such as Alex Haley's *Roots* and Thomas Keneally's *Schindler's List.* The authors of these works wrote meaningful and interesting books that were essentially reports on difficult, painful, even horrifying topics. (This is not to say you have to write about topics that make most people sad, or that the only good writing is writing about serious, heavy topics. Many upbeat topics can spark worthwhile writing, too.)

Think of a problem you once faced or a difficulty you overcame. Think of the feelings you had about that subject: anger, fear, disappointment, hope, excitement, determination. Did you solve this problem? If so, how? Maybe others would benefit from your experience. Writing about the problem and its solution might make a great report.

Newspapers and magazines can also provide topic ideas. Pick one up and flip through the pages. Look at the pictures, titles of articles, and even the advertisements. You will find lots of topic ideas. For example, an advertisement for a vacation spot might prompt the following ideas:

➤ Family Vacations Can Lead to Family Feuds
➤ People Living in Far-Off Places Have Different Customs Than Americans
➤ The Best Vacations Don't Have to Cost a Lot
➤ The Worst/Best Vacation I Ever Had
➤ The Ten Best Things About Traveling by Air/Boat/Car
➤ My Secret Remedy for Airsickness/Seasickness/Carsickness
➤ Things the Government Should Do to Make Travel Safer

Ideas can also come from your school textbooks. Both words and pictures can inspire ideas. Encyclopedias and other reference books can do the same. When using one of these sources to generate ideas, ask yourself these questions: Why do I want to write about this? What do I already know about this subject? What do I want to learn? How do I feel about this?

Books of quotations can inspire you. Select a quotation with which you strongly agree or disagree. Ask yourself: Do I think it's true or false? Have I had experiences I can write about to back up my feeling? Can I restate the quotation in my own words? Can I illustrate a quotation with an experience of my own? The answers to all of these questions can generate ideas for your writing. (See the Appendix for a list of quotations you can use in your own writing.)

Think about anything currently popular or trendy, such as collectibles, television programs, movies, or celebrities. Special events in your community, or even that old standby, the weather, can be a source of inspiration. But always remember: The entire writing process will be much more interesting, valuable, and fun if you choose a topic that interests you.

Developing Your Topic

Now that you know where your inspiration is coming from, the next step is to brainstorm about it, record it on paper, and start developing it as a topic. You can do this by jotting your thoughts down in a list, writing down anything that comes to mind when you think of your topic. Let your ideas flow, no matter how silly they seem. If you have an idea connected to your topic that you're unsure of, write it as a question. The important thing is to keep the ideas flowing. This is one time when neatness doesn't count!

Sample Topic List for a Report on Beavers:

Topic: beavers
Size: about 70 pounds, 2–3 feet long!
Habitat: slow-moving streams near wooded areas
Teeth are orange!
Eat bark. Eat wood?
Build dams
Swim underwater 25 min-
   utes at a time without
   breathing!
Webbed feet, like a duck
Tail like a paddle
Once hunted for their fur
Who are their enemies?

Or, you may want to try putting your thoughts on paper in another form. One common type of "graphic aid" is a word web.

When you make a list, you jot your main idea at the top of the page and list your thoughts underneath it. With a word web, you write your main idea in the center of the page and write your ideas around it as they occur to you, joining the words to the main idea with lines.

Each one of the topics in the circles of the web can become the subject of the topic sentence of a paragraph in your report. The topic in the middle circle can become your title. (For more information on topic sentences, see Chapter 6.)

One reason it's good to jot your ideas down quickly in graphic form is that it "fixes" them in place so you won't have to risk losing them from your memory when it comes time to write your report. But another reason word webs are useful prewriting tools is that they help you "see" your ideas, allowing you to notice connections you might have missed if you relied only on your memory.

It works like this: As you write each item on your word web or list, that item can help you think of even more items. (When you look at the sample word web and list on these pages, you can probably think of many other items you could add to each.) With a word web, especially, lines drawn between items show how they are related. These lines can help you when it's time to organize your report, because it's easy to see which items should be written about first, second, and so on.

Once you've finished with your list or web, look it over. Put it down for a while, and then read it again. If you think of more details to add, go ahead. A web or list that is rich in details indicates that you have a topic that's worth writing about. (If your list is pretty small, you can always begin again with another topic!)

Sample word web based on a news article in a local paper

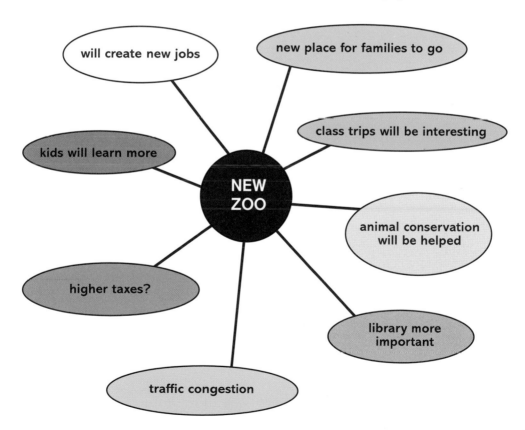

Charts can also help you think of ideas. Suppose you are thinking of writing a description of something for your report. Write the subject you will be describing at the top of a piece of paper. Underneath, create a chart with five columns, one for each of the five senses. Write appropriate details in each column.

Creating a chart like this gives you plenty of details to write about for your topic: family holiday celebrations. Or, it can help you de-

cide to focus your report on just one of the topics listed.

For example, look at the "Touching" column. Reading about the "Hard, uncomfortable chairs at the kids' table in the kitchen," you might

Family Holiday Celebrations

SEEING	HEARING	TASTING	SMELLING	TOUCHING
• Decorations	• Traditional music, like Christmas carols	• Moist turkey and stuffing	• Savory turkey roasting	• New baby cousin's soft cheek
• Family members in fancy clothing	• Sounds of football game on TV	• Sweet pumpkin pie everyone likes; strange mincemeat pie no one likes	• Onion-y stuffing	• Hard, un-comfortable chairs at kids' table in the kitchen
• Mom's "good" dishes and silverware	• Uncles arguing about sports; aunts laughing at old stories	• Lumpy mashed potatoes with deli-cious brown gravy	• Spicy pies	• Dry turkey overcooked by Grandma
• Cousins you haven't seen in ages	• Little cousins running around	• Bitter broccoli	• Fruity cider	• Grandpa's rough beard when you kiss his cheek
	• Sounds of video games from den		• Fresh seasonal flowers	
			• Sharp cheese	
			• Hearty gravy	
			• Aunt Mara's overpower-ing perfume	
			• Uncle Ralph's familiar aftershave	

decide to change the topic of your report from a general report on "Family Holiday Celebrations" to "How Kids Feel About Sitting at the Kids' Table at Family Holiday Celebrations."

To develop this topic, you might take a survey of your friends and classmates, asking, "Does your family celebrate holidays such as Christmas and Thanksgiving, or similar holidays from a different culture? If these celebrations include a big meal, do you have to sit at a kids' table? How do you feel about that?" (Don't forget to include in your notes how *you* feel about it.) "Will you have a kids' table at your family get-togethers when you're grown up? Why or why not?" As your questions are answered, jot down the answers in another list, web, or chart. Now you've got a great topic with lots of details for an interesting report.

Now that you've got your topic and you've begun to develop it, you're ready to think about one more prewriting task: determining your audience and purpose for writing.

Why Are You Writing?

All writers write for a purpose. Every time you write—whether it's to provide information, to persuade readers of your point of view, to entertain the reader, or simply to express your own feelings and ideas—ask yourself: What am I trying to accomplish?

It's true that, as a student, your main reason for writing might be "because my teacher told me to." Even if that's your main reason, ask yourself: How can I write to fulfill this assignment?

If your teacher has asked you to write a report on a social studies topic or a book you've read, chances are she's looking for an informational report. If your assignment is to report on your opinion of an issue, you are probably going to be writing a persuasive report. If you are writing a report on an experience, or if you are writing on a theme, then your purpose will be to entertain. (Entertaining writing doesn't have to be funny. Some of the most popular and entertaining professional writers specialize in frightening readers or touching their deepest emotions and making them cry!)

You can have more than one reason for writing. Perhaps you want to entertain and inform your audience. Let's say you are writing a report on your summer vacation in the mountains. You might blend funny experiences (falling into a stream, getting "eaten alive" by insects) with facts about the mountains, such as their height, physical characteristics, animals that inhabit them, and so on. Whatever reason you choose for writing your report, it's important to choose at least one.

Having a reason for your writing helps your personality come through in your words. If there are 26 kids in your class, and each one is writing about the first day of school, there are 26 different ways that that experience can be written about. You see things differently from everyone else, and it's that unique vision that will make your writing unmistakably yours.

Who Is Your Audience?

For a school writing assignment, your audience is probably your teacher and perhaps (especially if your report is to be an oral report) your classmates. (If you were writing a letter, your audience would be the person to whom the letter is addressed; if you were writing a journal entry, your audience would be yourself.)

Whoever your audience is, before you begin to write, ask yourself:
➤ What does my audience already know about this subject?
➤ What might they want to know?
➤ What do I want to tell them?

The answers to these questions will help you decide what information to include and exclude as you write. For example, if you were writing a class report on a candidate running for president of the United States, you would probably realize that your teacher already knows that the

United States is a democracy in which people elect a new president every four years. You wouldn't have to mention this fact in your report. However, your audience might want to know information about the current candidates' positions and accomplishments, as well as your opinion on the better candidate for the job.

In a report on elections, you might also want to compare and contrast two candidates. Comparison and contrast is another popular style of report writing. It can be used to write about all sorts of topics, from foods to historic figures to hobbies. Comparing and contrasting, persuading, informing, entertaining: These are among the most common purposes for writing. Knowing what your purpose is will help you write a better report.

It's also very important to know your audience when you're writing a report. Knowing who will be reading or listening to your report will help you select the right language to use in your writing. For example, if you were writing a story for young children, you would use small words and short, simple sentences. You wouldn't confuse them by including too many details. But if you were writing a letter to the editor of the local newspaper, you could use longer sentences and more difficult words. You could include lots of details to support your main ideas, your sentences could be more complex, and your language would probably be more formal.

Now that you have selected your topic, know what details you need to include, know your purpose for writing, and know who your audience is, you're ready to move on to the research stage of the writing process. This is where you begin to add "muscle" to the skinny frame of a topic, creating a "super-strong" report. Let's get busy!

Checklist for Starting the Writing Process

- ❑ Did I generate a large number of ideas by:
  - •looking through my personal journal?
  - •thinking of a problem or difficulty I once faced?
  - •looking through newspapers or magazines?
  - •looking through school reading or text books?
  - •looking through books of quotations?
- ❑ Did I ask myself the following questions when generating ideas:
  - •Why do I want to write about this?
  - •What do I already know about this subject?
  - •What do I want to learn?
  - •How do I feel about this?
- ❑ Did I capture my ideas on paper in one of the following forms:
  - •a list
  - •a word web
  - •a chart
- ❑ Did I think of many details about my topic?
- ❑ Do I know my audience?
- ❑ Do I know my purpose for writing?*

*Of course, one purpose for writing is "Because my teacher told me I had to." But that's not what is meant here by "purpose for writing." Your purpose for writing is what you want your report to do: persuade, give your opinion, compare and contrast two things, and so on.

Research

Research is a funny word. It sounds like it means "search again."
What it really means is to look for details that will support the topic
you've chosen to write about.

There are lots of different kinds of supporting details—and lots of
places to look for them. The ones you select will depend on what
kind of report you're writing. In this chapter, we'll look at the kinds
of details first and then look at where to find them.

Kinds of Details

Facts A fact is a statement that
can be proved to be true. "The
Taj Mahal is in India" is a fact. A
fact can be checked and proved,
either by direct observation and
verification (written or photo-
graphic), consultation with primary sources (eyewitnesses), or
by looking in reference sources,
such as encyclopedias, published
reports, nonfiction books, or
directories.

Opinions "The Taj Mahal is the most beautiful building in the
world" is not a fact; it is an opinion. There is no way to prove that
the Taj Mahal is more beautiful than all other buildings, because
beauty means different things to different people. Whether or not
a thing is beautiful is a matter of opinion. When writing your opinions in a report, you must be careful to support them with facts.

Reasons Did you ever ask your parents for permission to do something and then give logical explanations to persuade them that you
should be allowed to do it? If so, you already know something about

reasons. Reasons are logical arguments for or against a subject. For example, if you want permission to go to see *Space Aliens Among Us!* at the local movie theater, you might try giving the following reasons:

Reasons to See Space Aliens Among Us!

REASON

"It's scientific, about space!"

"The movie director is a creative genius"

"It's half price today"

"All my friends' parents are letting them go!"

POSSIBLE REACTION

Might work, especially if your parents believe in aliens. Sounds like it could be true.

Also might work. Makes you sound intelligent and artistic.

Might work. Parents do like a bargain.

Never use this one. Parents instantly respond with "I'm not 'all your friends' parents!' The only one I'm concerned with is YOU!"

As you can see, some reasons are better than others! The same is true when writing reports. For example, let's say you looked through the local newspaper to get topic ideas. You noticed an article about an animal shelter that was going to be shut down. You decided the topic of your report would be the importance of keeping the shelter open.

In your report, you would give your opinion ("I think the shelter should be kept open because . . ."), and then use logical arguments and reasons to support your opinion. You would research how important animal shelters are to communities, find out about all the good they do, and how much damage can be done to people and property by abandoned animals in communities where shelters are not available. Those would all be good reasons to support your opinion, and they would make your report strong. (Just writing, "I think the shelter should stay open because I love kittens and puppies," would not be an example of an opinion supported by good reasons.)

Examples
These are instances of something that you use in your writing to support a point. Taking the example of the animal shelter, above, you could do research to find examples of communities that used new and different ways to raise money to keep their animal shelters open. Including these examples in your report will strengthen it. In addition, you could also do research to find examples of problems that occur when communities don't have animal shelters.

Sensory Details
These add interest to your report by telling how things look, taste, feel, smell, and sound. In the animal shelter report, for example, you might include sensory details that tell how the animals look—their sizes, shapes, colors, and conditions. You'd want to add the sounds of the shelter—the yips, woofs, barks, yelps, meows, and purrs. The clanging sounds of cages and gates, the tones of voice used by the animals' caretakers, and the loving words of people adopting the sheltered pets would also be good sensory details to include.

Stories or Events
Your report might include a story retelling an event that supports your opinion. In the case of the animal shelter report, you might consider including the story of a dog that was adopted from a shelter and given to a lonely old man, becoming that old man's best friend and his only connection to the rest of the

community. A story like that would support your opinion that animal shelters do a lot of good for their neighborhoods. Where do all these supporting details come from? Research.

Where Do You Find Sources for Research?

There are many places to find support for your opinions, including:

The Library
The librarian will be happy to help you find books, magazines, newspapers, encyclopedias, and other reference sources. It's important to know how to look up information once you find the reference books that contain the facts you need. Knowing how reference books are arranged can help you find facts quickly and easily. Check out the box below for help.

Reference books are specially designed so that it's easy for you to locate the information they contain. Most reference books include:

Copyright page—tells you when the book was printed. This helps you know if the information the book contains is up-to-date or out-of-date.

Table of contents—tells what the chapters are about and on what pages they start.

Appendix—if there is one, it comes after the main portion of the book. It may contain charts, maps, illustrations, diagrams, or extra information about the author or subject.

Glossary—found at the back of the book, it lists special or difficult words contained in the body of the book, defines them, and sometimes tells how to pronounce them.

Index—an alphabetical list of special words and names that are found in a book. It lists all the pages where those words can be found. In a book about beavers, for example, the index would probably contain words such as "dam," "lodge," "teeth," and "fur."

Bibliography—lists books or articles that helped the author in writing the book. (You might also want to look up some of the books listed in the bibliography of any reference book you are reading to get additional details.)

Interviews You can get lots of primary source information by interviewing people who are in a position to know firsthand about your topic. For your animal shelter report, for example, you might interview local politicians or workers at the shelter, or even people who have adopted pets there.

An interview involves more than just asking a few simple questions. You have to be prepared to ask the right questions when you interview a source. Questions that can be answered with a "yes" or "no" are usually not very useful for the report writer. For example:

> Student: "Are you glad you got your dog from the Parkdale Animal Shelter?"
>
> Subject: "Yes."

See? There's not much detail there to add to your report. But if you pose your questions a little differently, you'll probably get more useful answers.

> Student: "How different has your life been since you got your pet from the Parkdale Animal Shelter?"
>
> Subject: "Oh, it is different in so many ways! Before, I had no reason to get out of bed in the morning. Now, I know Muffin needs me to fix his breakfast and take him to the park. Before Muffin came into my life, I felt no

---

Primary Sources

Primary sources are the people who witnessed or participated in an event, or who recorded their reactions to it immediately after it happened. (Records don't have to be written; they can include photographs, videotapes, computer disks, or audio recordings.)

Primary sources are not necessarily more reliable than secondary sources (reference materials like books, newspapers, magazines, Web pages, and filmed accounts that were written based on the primary source's evidence). You have to check carefully when using primary source material, perhaps speaking to more than one participant or witness to get the complete picture.

one cared about me. . . . I was so lonely. Now, I have someone with me all the time who is happy to see me, who is always there to comfort me, and who guards me and makes me feel safe. Muffin has become my best pal!"

There's plenty of detail there for your report!

Newspapers and magazines are great places to see examples of good interview questions. Make a habit of reading them and taking note of the kinds of questions the reporters ask. See the box below for samples of interview questions you can use as a model for your own interviews.

Asking questions that begin with words and phrases like "When did," "How long," "What's the most/the best/the worst/your favorite," and "What do you want people to know about" can lead to interesting, detail-rich answers. You might want to prepare and take to your interview a sheet of lined paper on which you've written questions using these phrases. Be sure you leave spaces between each question so you can write down the subject's answers. Even if you

Sample interview question starters (fill in the blanks with words that relate to the topic of the interview—the subject's job, an experience, or an event that happened to him or her):

"What's the best thing about _(being an animal-shelter vet)?_"
"When did you first _(realize how important shelters are)?_"
"Was there ever a time when you wanted _(to quit)?_"
"What would you like people to know about _(the importance of animal shelters in our communities)?_"

plan to capture the subject's answers on audio or video tape, it's good to have your questions written down beforehand. You can always ask more questions as they occur to you during the interview. But having a list beforehand keeps the interview on target, and it can help you get the answers you need for your report.

Searching for Other Sources

You might be surprised to discover all the resources available to help you with your research. Here's a list of some. You may think of others.

almanacs
dictionaries
Internet sites
atlases
magazines
audiotapes

encyclopedias
maps
books
field trips
museums
CD-ROMs

films
directories (e.g.,
phone books)
television programs
textbooks

The Internet

The Internet is loaded with Web sites that can provide information. The great thing about the Internet is that it's chock-full of informa-

HANDY TIP:

A search engine (like Yahoo!) is a service provided by a company that employs a lot of people who work to sort through Web sites and index them. When you type in the key word you're searching for, the search engine can pull up and show you many of the Web sites they have indexed on that subject. Using a search engine can save you lots of time when doing research on the Web.

tion that has been placed there by all kinds of people and organizations. Unfortunately, that's also the down side of the Internet. There's so much information it can be hard to find just what you're looking for. Because anyone with a computer can set up a Web site, it's also hard to be sure just how reliable the information is that you find on the Internet.

Here are some Web sites that have proven their value to students and other writers:

The Presidential Libraries

http://www.nara.gov/nara/ president/address/html

National History Day

http://www.thehistorynet.com/ NationalHistoryDay/

The Library of Congress

http://www.loc.gov/

The White House

http://www.whitehouse.gov/WH/Welcome.html

Repositories of Primary Sources

http://www.uidaho.edu/special-collections/Other.
Repositories.html

Map Quest

http://www.mapquest.com/

Franklin Institute of Science Museum

http://sin.fi.edu/tfi/welcome.html

Resources at the Smithsonian Institution

http://www.si.edu/resource/start/htm.

No matter what kind of reference materials you use to prepare your report, the following checklist can help you make sure you get the most out of them.

Research Checklist

❑ Did I use more than one source of information: book/Web site/ newspaper/magazine? (Try to use more than two books, or, if possible, at least one of each of the above sources, to make sure you get a wide variety of details for your report.)

❑ Did I check the copyright dates of the books or videos I used? The dates of the magazines and newspapers? If the books were written more than ten years ago, did I try to find more recent information?

❑ Did I write down the title, author, copyright date, and publisher of all the books I used?

❑ Did I write down the publication date of any newspapers or magazines I used?

❑ Did I take note of the name of any Web site I used?

❑ Did I write down the title, director, producer, writer, copyright date, and production house of any films/videos I used?

❑ Did I write down the full names of any people I interviewed?

Taking Notes

You've chosen your topic, you've brainstormed details, you know your audience and your purpose for writing, and you've selected and studied your research materials. Now, how do you begin turning that research into writing? You start by taking notes.

Learning how to take thorough research notes will help you create well-written reports that are filled with details. Details make the difference between a skimpy, boring, poorly written report that won't keep your teacher's interest for the time it takes to read it (or your listeners' interest for the time it takes you to present it) and a substantial, interesting report that's actually fun to read (and write)!

Knowing a few things before you begin will help you take useful notes. The main thing to remember about notes is to keep them short. Say you're writing a report on Christopher Columbus, and one of your reference books says: "Christopher Columbus set sail from Spain and discovered the New World in 1492." Your notes should only say something like: "Columbus, Spain to America, 1492."

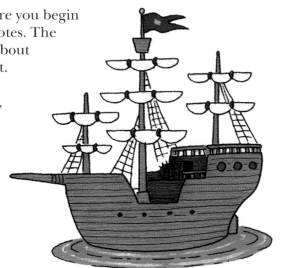

Although they should be short, they should also include the important facts. Important facts are usually those that tell about the sub-

---

Things to remember when taking notes:
• Keep them short, but include important points.
• Write them in your own words; don't copy them directly from your resource.

ject (who) and answer the questions what, where, when, why, and how. These are called the Five Ws and H, and we'll talk more about them later in this chapter.

How to Take Notes

You can write notes on a pad of paper, separate loose-leaf sheets, or index cards. Some people prefer index cards and loose-leaf sheets because they can physically rearrange them when using them later to create an outline. With practice, you will find the method you like best. Whatever works for you is the method you should use. After all, your notes are a tool for you; no one else is going to see them.

Another thing to remember about notes is that they should be in your own words, not the words of the author of the reference book. Finding your own ways to rephrase what the author is saying is a challenge, but it's the only way to develop your own unique voice as a writer.

One way to get some practice putting ideas into different words is to try playing a game called "In Other Words" with some friends. Whenever one of you makes a statement, the other tries to say it in other words. For example, your friend says, "The 1998 New York Yankees were the greatest baseball team of all time!" You say, "Three years before the beginning of the third millennium, the American League team from the Big Apple proved themselves superior to all others throughout baseball history!" The game continues until one of you is stumped and cannot put the same thought into any other words.

It's a silly game, but it can help you learn an important skill that can serve you well when writing all kinds of reports. Rephrasing another writer's words in your own words (called "paraphrasing") also helps "fix" the thoughts in your mind. It also helps you make sure you really understand those thoughts. Just parroting or copying another writer's words doesn't demonstrate any learning on your part. And as if that weren't enough, copying another writer's words without giving that writer credit is really stealing. You wouldn't want someone else taking credit for your ideas; you don't want to take credit for someone else's. And your teachers don't assign reports to see how well you can copy other people's ideas out of books. Reports are supposed to give your teacher an idea of how you think, and a report can't do that if it's in someone else's words.

Suppose that, in order to prove a point in your report, you absolutely have to include the words of another writer in your report. Well, you can do that if you give that writer credit. Make sure you surround all the words written by someone else in quotation marks. Before you start the quote, announce to the reader that what's coming up was written by another author, and mention the author's name. Tell where you found the quote, and, if the quote is longer than four lines, set it off from the rest of your writing by putting an extra line of space before and after it.

In the immortal words of William Shakespeare in his play, *Hamlet,* "Neither a borrower, Nor a lender, be." Especially when it comes to words! (In case you didn't notice, that's an example of how to use another writer's words in your own writing! Notice the introduction of the author, his work, and the use of quotation marks. It's that easy!)

Organizing Your Notes

In the beginning of this chapter, you
read about how to find the important details in a reference source by asking and
answering a series of questions known as "The Five
Ws and H." They are

Who?
What?
When?
Where?
Why?
How?

It takes some practice to pick the Five Ws and H out of an article
or story. One way to practice is to try picking them out of a familiar
story, like a fairy tale or fable. The story of Goldilocks and the
Three Bears is one most students know. It's retold below so you can
practice picking out the Five Ws and H. Read the story and circle
the answers to the questions Who, What, When, Where, Why, and
How. Write which question the sentence answers in small letters

Who?

What?

Why?

Where?

When?

How?

near your circles. Then compare your answers with those on the chart printed below the story.

Goldilocks and the Three Bears: A Crime Story

Once upon a time, in a cottage in the middle of the deep, dark forest, there lived a family of brown bears. There was Mama Bear, Papa Bear, and Baby Bear. One day, when they sat down to eat their midday meal of porridge, the bears noticed that it was too hot to eat right away. "I know," said Papa Bear, "let's go for a walk until it cools." And so they left the three bowls of porridge to cool on the wooden table.

Now it so happened that in this forest there also lived a pretty little girl. She was named Goldilocks because of her beautiful, golden hair. Unfortunately, Goldilocks was as full of mischief as she was pretty. She had been told not to go near the bears' cottage and not to touch things that didn't belong to her, but she didn't always do what she was told.

The day the bears took their walk, Goldilocks was also out walking in the forest. Seeing the bears' cottage, she walked up and looked through the window. "Nobody's home," she thought to herself. So she just walked up to the door and entered, without even knocking.

Seeing the three bowls of porridge on the table, she ate a little bit from one. "Too hot," she said. She tried another. "Too cold," she said, and tried another. "Just right," she said, and ate it all up.

She tried out the bears' chairs, too. "Too hard," she said, trying one. "Too soft," she said, trying another. "Just right," she said, and whoops! The little chair broke into pieces!

By this time, Goldilocks was tired. She went upstairs and tried out the bears' beds. Again, the first was too hard, the second too soft, but the third was just right! It was so comfortable that she fell asleep, and she was still sleeping when the bears came home. Seeing their porridge eaten and their chair broken, they thought, "We've been robbed! Maybe the burglar is still here and we can catch him!" Carefully, they went upstairs to see if the intruder was still there.

"There she is, in my bed," cried Baby Bear. Goldilocks woke up in alarm, threw off the covers, jumped out of the window, and ran home. She never went back to that cottage again!

A "Five Ws and H" Chart for Goldilocks and the Three Bears:

Who: Goldilocks; Mama, Papa, and Baby Bear

What: A crime

When: Once upon a time...

Where: The bears' cottage in the forest

Why: Goldilocks has a tendency to go places and do things without permission.

How: She entered the bears' house while they were out. When they returned, they were shocked to find her sleeping there and their property broken and ruined.

You might also notice that many articles printed in your local newspaper are written in this Five Ws and H style. For more practice, try this exercise: Take the first five pages from your local newspaper and select any three stories that interest you. Circle the first paragraph in each story. You should be able, within the first paragraph, to find the answers to the questions Who, What, When, and Where. Sometimes you'll have to read further to find out the Why and How. Notice how the newspaper writers get the important details into the beginning of their articles and then spend the next few paragraphs explaining and supporting those details. In a way, that's what you will be doing with your reports: setting out your main idea and then supporting it with details in a well-organized way.

Creating a Note-Taking Grid

One way to organize the details you've collected after asking the Five Ws and H is to create a note-taking grid. This is an excellent way to organize all your notes so you have them at your fingertips when preparing the outline for your report. Yes, it does mean re-writing all the notes you scribbled on loose-leaf paper or index

cards. But the time you spend re-writing your notes on the grid will
be well worth it when it comes to writing your actual report, because
not only does this method organize your notes, it arranges them in
the form in which you'll probably want to use them when writing
your final report.

Look at this sample note-taking grid for a report on Dr. Martin
Luther King, Jr. By filling in each section of the grid, the writer of
this report has a head start on organizing his or her rough draft.
All the facts are in order, and the resource materials where the facts
were found are right there, ready to be included in the report
(maybe even for extra credit!).

Subject of Report:
Dr. Martin Luther King, Jr.

RESOURCES	Book, *Meet Dr. King* by Mildred Allgoog, 1986, Apogee Press.	Movie, *The Content of His Character,* made in 1990 by Zenith Films, directed by Alva Barlsow
WHO?	Son of preacher, he grew up to be a preacher	One of the greatest leaders of all time
WHAT?	Civil rights leader	Influenced the lawmakers and the average citizens
WHEN?	1960s	1960s
WHERE?	Mississippi; Alabama; Washington, D.C.	All across the U.S., especially the deep South
WHY?	He felt African Americans weren't treated fairly	To bring equal protection of law to all people, so his kids could have a better life
HOW?	He led marches, made speeches	Used only nonviolent methods

When you prepare your report, refer to the notes you wrote on index cards or paper to help you fill in the grid. In the first box next to the word "Resources," write the complete name of the first resource you'll be using (whether it's a book, movie, interview, or other source), including all publishing information. Then go down to the next box under the "Who" heading. Ask yourself, who did this resource talk about? Look for the answer in your notes.

Continue down that column, writing the answers to the remaining Five Ws and H questions that you discovered in that particular resource. Not every question will have an answer. For example, if you're writing a report on African elephants, you may not have an answer to the Who question. However, you will be able to fill in answers to the What, When, Where, and Why questions. The How questions are not always answered, either. That's okay. Not every topic has a "How." Use the completed grid on the previous page as a model.

Use Two Grids to Create a Compare/Contrast Report

As you might imagine, if you want to create a report that compares and contrasts two topics, you can use this method to prepare two grids—one for each topic.

Persuade With a Grid

If you want to use a grid to prepare a persuasive report, start out with a blank grid and write your opinion on the top of the page. This will be the topic of your report.

This time when you ask yourself the Five Ws and H, you might not find all the answers in your notes. Some of the answers should be supported by research you've written in your notes, but the rest should come from your own thoughts and feelings. Alternate writing information from resources and from your own opinions, as in the sample grid that follows.

Topic: Our Animal Shelter Should Not Be Closed

RESOURCES	*The Daily Citizen,* (newspaper) March 18, 1998	My opinion	My grandpa, interview
WHO	Ed Rubenstein, dog catcher	Everybody in our community	John Coombes
WHAT	Has made a study of animal shelters across the nation that showed cases of rabies in dog populations rise 50 percent when shelters are closed	Should be concerned. Rabies is a serious disease that can kill. We should fight to keep the shelters open.	Thinks shelters should be shut down because they're smelly, noisy, and messy
WHEN	All during the 1990s	Especially now, with politicians talking about closing the shelter	Should be shut soon
WHERE	In cities the same size as ours	Right here in our town	Especially the one near his house
WHY	He was concerned about the effects of closing shelters	To protect ourselves and our pets	To let the neighbors get a good night's sleep
HOW	He looked up his fellow dog catchers in the Directory of American Dog Catchers and asked them to send him reports on the subject	By writing letters, signing petitions, and staging peaceful protests in front of the shelter	Just pass a law against them, lock the doors, fire the workers, let the animals go free, hopefully to other neighborhoods

Whichever method you use, once you've filled in your grid, look it over. With all your facts laid out in this form, it should be easy for you to decide which are most important and which are not so important, which should definitely be included in your report and which you might want to do without. (Can you pick the opinions in the grid on the previous page that probably should not be included in your report? If you said Grandpa's interview, you're right.)

Now it's up to you to decide which bits of information should go first in your outline and which should follow. Seeing all your research, details, opinions, facts, and reasons collected in this manner should really help you with the next stage of the writing process: creating an outline.

HANDY TIP:

When using research materials—such as books, magazines, and newspapers—that belong to the school or public library, you must never write in them or circle anything in them. The problem then is, how do you mark the sentences and paragraphs you want to remember to write about for your notes? You can use small self-stick notes. Attach the note to the page near the sentence you want to remember for your notes, and then write on the self-stick note to remind yourself which of the Five Ws or H the sentence answers, or include any other information you might want to remember.

Creating an Outline

An outline is the framework that supports your report. A good outline helps you make sure you don't forget a single thought you want to express in your finished report. Using your note-taking grid as a reference, you can make sure you include all the important details that your research uncovered. Putting them into an outline helps you make sure that nothing you had wanted to include is left out of your finished report.

There are several different ways to organize your outline. For example, if you are reporting on an event in history, you will need to review your note-taking grid to discover what happened first, what happened second, and so on. This is a sequential or chronological report. It's very easy to organize. In fact, this kind of report almost organizes itself.

| Dinosaurs roamed the Earth. | Dinosaurs became extinct. | Today, scientists try to find out why. |

But let's say you're writing a report that describes something. Perhaps it's a work of art, an animal, or a sports hero. In that case, you'll need to decide the order in which to write your descriptive report.

You'll need to write the ideas in a sequence that makes sense and enables the reader to understand what you are describing. If you are describing an animal, for example, you might want to start your report with a description of how the animal is born, move on to how it grows, and finish with how it lives as an adult.

If you are describing a sports hero, you might talk about his or her most recent achievements and work your way back to the beginning of his or her career. Or, you can start your description at the beginning of your hero's career and move to the present. It's up to you. Whichever you choose, just make sure to stick with that choice. (You might confuse your reader if you move back and forth between time periods when describing your topic.)

When you look over your notes to decide in what order you want to put your details, it helps to think: Can I organize these details from biggest to smallest? Best to worst? Nearest to farthest? Most important to least important? Most recent to most distant?

If you used a note-taking grid, you can now go back and, using a different color pen or pencil than the one you used to write your notes, number each detail in the order in which you want to write about it (figure 1).

figure 1

If you didn't use the note-taking grid, but you took notes on paper in a list or a word-web format, go back over them and number them the same way (figure 2). If you took your notes on index cards, go through them and physically arrange them in the order in which you want them (figure 3). Now you're just about ready to write your outline.

figure 2

figure 3

Several Ways to Organize Your Outline

Depending upon the kind of report you are going to write, there are several different ways to organize your outline. For the chronological or sequential report, decide if you will begin with the event that happened first or last, and arrange your outline accordingly.

Chronological or Sequential Report Outline

Dinosaurs

I. Introduction: What happened to dinosaurs?

II. Dinosaurs roamed the Earth

    a. Scientists found fossils, show existence of dinosaurs

    b. Fossils found all over Earth, every continent

    c. Scientists can tell age of dinosaur fossils. They know when dinosaurs lived.

III. Dinosaurs became extinct

    a. At a certain point in time, fossils stopped

    b. No dinosaurs today

IV. Scientists try to find out why

    a. Many doing research

    b. Lots of theories, no real answer

V. Conclusion: My opinion based on reported information

This sample outline shows how a chronological or sequential report might be organized. Notice how each main idea follows in time from the distant past (when dinosaurs roamed the earth) to the present (when scientists study them), and ends with the writer giving her opinion at the conclusion.

Notice also that the outline is not really written in complete sentences, just sketchy phrases. The sketchy phrases will be turned into complete sentences during the rough draft phase of the writing process. Both the main ideas and details in the outline come from the research that was organized in the note-taking grid, word web, and/or index cards (see figures 1–3 on page 42).

Comparison and Contrast Report Outline

For a report in which you compare and contrast two ideas or items, the outline will look pretty much the same as the sequential or chronological outline on the previous page. You will use Roman numerals for the main

ideas and letters of the alphabet for the supporting details. You'll start with an introduction that states your goal: to show how two items are alike or different.

Examples of comparison and contrast reports might be:

• Our Modern World Is Much Like Ancient Rome. This report outline would start out with a topic sentence stating that life in

America today is not so different from life in ancient Rome. Then, Roman-numeral headings would name several areas of life, such as family, work, and school. Each of these headings would be followed by supporting details—

When writing comparison and contrast reports and outlines, make sure you state all the similarities together and all the differences together. For example, in a report giving your opinion on "Who's the Better Fighter: Mohammed Ali or Mike Tyson?" you might say:

"Mike Tyson and Mohammed Ali are both boxers. They have both been heavyweight champions. They have earned millions of dollars from their skills in the ring, but their similarities end there. Muhammed Ali is the much greater athlete. . ." Then you'd list and discuss the differences. Don't go back and forth between similarities and differences, or you'll confuse the reader.

lettered a, b, c, and so on—to illustrate the point of the report: that life today is like life in ancient Rome.

• Muhammed Ali Is a Better Fighter Than Mike Tyson. This report outline would start out with an introduction stating the topic. Then the Roman-numeral headings would probably list several characteristics of what it takes to be a great fighter. The a, b, and c headings underneath would be followed by supporting details to show the writer's opinion that Muhammed Ali possesses these qualities and that Mike Tyson does not.

• People Speak English in England . . . Only They Don't Sound Like Us! The introduction of this report would state the writer's opinion that the English spoken in England doesn't sound like American English. The Roman-numeral headings would point out several differences in vocabulary and pronunciation, and the a, b, and c headings underneath would be followed by examples that the writer has researched by interviewing subjects or reading reference books.

Questions to Ask Yourself When Preparing Your Outline

No matter what kind of report you are planning to write—sequential, comparison and contrast, persuasive, descriptive—there are several questions you should ask yourself as you complete your outline.

1. Is my topic sentence clearly stated in my report's introduction? Would someone picking up this report know what I'm going to write about just by looking at my topic sentence in my outline?

2. Is my information arranged in a way that is easy to follow? Does it jump around between time periods, or does it progress smoothly in sequence?

3. If I'm comparing and contrasting two things, did I state all the similarities together and all the differences together?

4. If I stated my opinion, did I support it with facts and details from my notes?

5. Did I end with a conclusion and give the reasons I came to that conclusion?

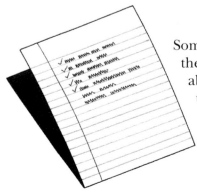

Alternative Forms of Outlines

Some students don't feel comfortable using the traditional kinds of outline described above. If it's all right with your teacher, there are some other kinds of outlines that you can use that might be better suited to your individual learning styles. Since some teachers do like to see your outlines as well as your finished reports, it may be a good idea to check with your teacher first to see if it's okay to use one of these alternative outline forms. (Note that although these alternative outline forms will help you organize your thoughts, they are not as useful for developing main ideas and supporting details as the traditional type of outline described above.)

Sequence Outline

You may be familiar with sequence outlines under their less fancy name: time lines. Sequence outlines or time lines are useful when writing reports for a social studies class, because they clearly show events in the order in which they took place.

As you can see, this kind of organization does not clearly show which are the main ideas and which are the supporting details. However, if you feel more comfortable using it, by all means give it a try. Just be sure it's okay with your teacher first, especially if he or she wants you to hand in your outline as well as your finished report for credit.

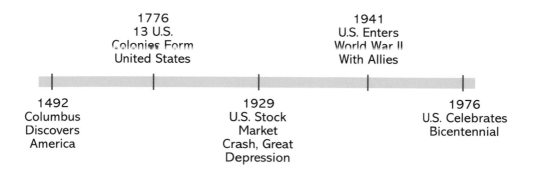

1776	1941
13 U.S.	U.S. Enters
Colonies Form	World War II
United States	With Allies

1492	1929	1976
Columbus	U.S. Stock	U.S. Celebrates
Discovers	Market	Bicentennial
America	Crash, Great	
	Depression	

Concept Outline

Concept outlines are similar to word webs. You start out by writing your main idea or topic sentence in the middle of a blank piece of paper, and then arrange your supporting details around it. Like the sequence outline, this type of outline does not make it as easy for you to see the relationships between the ideas as the traditional outline does, but many students feel comfortable with it. And if it's all right with your teacher, you may want to try using it.

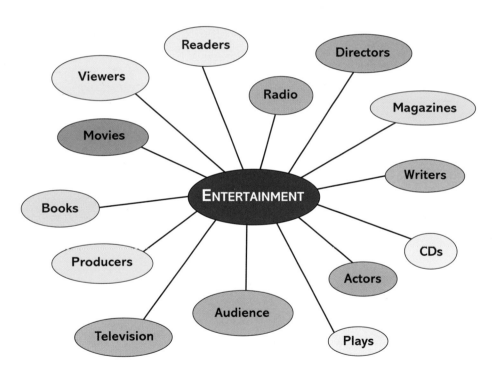

Flow-Chart Outline

This kind of outline is useful for showing the way one idea flows out of another.

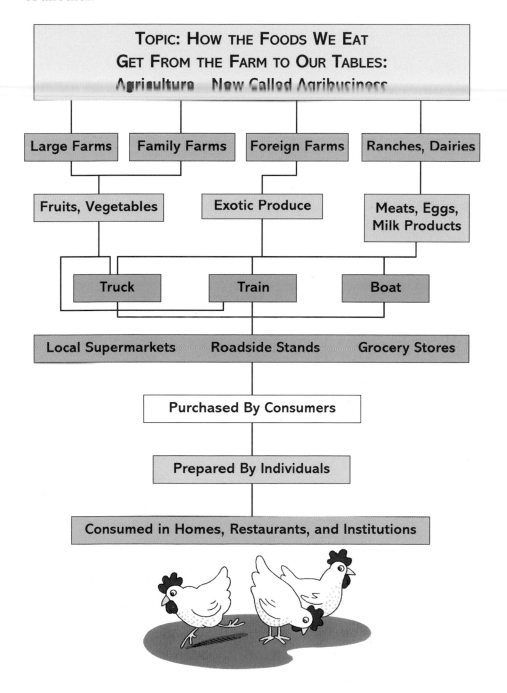

TOPIC: HOW THE FOODS WE EAT
GET FROM THE FARM TO OUR TABLES:
Agriculture — Now Called Agribusiness

| Large Farms | Family Farms | Foreign Farms | Ranches, Dairies |

Fruits, Vegetables — Exotic Produce — Meats, Eggs, Milk Products

Truck — Train — Boat

Local Supermarkets — Roadside Stands — Grocery Stores

Purchased By Consumers

Prepared By Individuals

Consumed in Homes, Restaurants, and Institutions

Venn Diagram Outlines

You are probably familiar with Venn diagrams from math classes. You can also use Venn diagrams to create outlines for reports, especially comparison and contrast reports. Once again, check with your teacher to see if this kind of outline is acceptable, especially if your teacher wants you to hand in your outline with your report for credit.

TOPIC: SKELETON BONES—COMPARE/CONTRAST

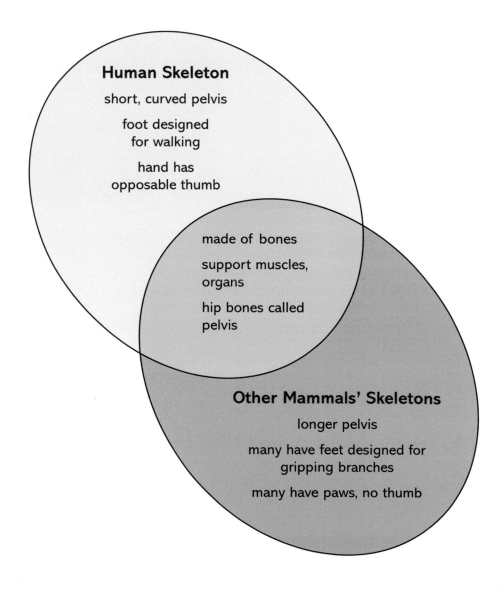

Human Skeleton

short, curved pelvis

foot designed
for walking

hand has
opposable thumb

made of bones

support muscles,
organs

hip bones called
pelvis

Other Mammals' Skeletons

longer pelvis

many have feet designed for
gripping branches

many have paws, no thumb

The aspects that are different about each topic are included in their separate circles. The things that are shared between the two topics are in the overlapping portion of their circles.

Whichever way you choose to outline your report, your outline should be a tool that lets you see clearly what your finished report is going to look like. Sometimes, when you finish writing your outline, you'll realize you haven't collected enough detail to make a really thorough report. Then you need to go back and do some more research before completing your outline and moving on to the next stage.

Right about now you're probably wondering why this is called the "prewriting" stage of the writing process! It seems like you've done an awful lot of writing already, doesn't it? Brainstorming ideas, turning those ideas into topics, searching for details, taking notes from research sources, interviewing subjects, and then creating note-taking grids and outlines...when, you must be wondering, do you actually start writing your report? Well, the good news is—soon! And when you do begin to write your rough draft, you'll find that all this prewriting pays off, making it easy for you to complete the best reports ever!

The Introduction and Rough Draft

You've followed the steps in the first five chapters and completed the prewriting portion of your report. You're now ready to begin the true "writing" portion of the writing process. Because of your careful note-taking and outlining, you know exactly what your report will include. Now, all you have to do is write it!

This can be easier said than done. After all, you can't just copy your sketchy notes. That wouldn't make much of a report. You certainly can't go back to your research and copy from your sources. That would be stealing. Whatever you write has to express the topic you've chosen in your own voice, thoughts, and ideas. It's easy to say "just write it in your own words." But what words? This is where knowing your audience comes in handy.

Since your audience is your classroom teacher and possibly your classmates, what you're aiming for when you begin to write your report is a balance between the formal language you probably found in your research materials, and the informal way you speak to your friends and family.

But don't worry too much about finding your voice right at this minute. You're still in the rough draft stage of the writing process, when you don't need to be concerned about writing perfect sentences in just the right voice. In the rough draft stage, the most important thing is to get your thoughts out of your outline, into sentence form, and into your report. Let's start with the basics.

Paragraphs: the Building Blocks of Reports

A report is composed of paragraphs. Each paragraph of a report tells about one topic. Each paragraph has a topic sentence and several other sentences that contain details supporting the topic sentence. And this is when your outline comes in handy. Each Roman numeral of your outline is going to be a paragraph or group of paragraphs in your report; each smaller division within that Roman numeral will be turned into one or a few sentences that support your topic sentence. Now it should be clear why you created your outline: You know exactly what information your paragraphs need to contain, and in what order those paragraphs should appear in your report. Remember, each paragraph only contains sentences that are necessary to support that one topic. (Notice the way all the sentences in this paragraph you're reading have to do with the contents of your paragraphs.)

Each sentence in a paragraph should be clear and make sense. The sentences should be complete and should flow smoothly. It's okay, however, to vary the length of the sentences; some can be long, some can be short. The sentences in a paragraph should be arranged in an order that leads the reader from one thought to another in a sensible manner so the reader doesn't get "lost." The sentences in the following paragraph are arranged in an order that does not make sense.

> **Goldilocks went for a walk in the woods. It was the cottage of the Three Bears. She saw a cottage. She went inside. She saw that the door was open. Goldilocks was curious.**

Could you put those sentences into an order that makes sense? Give it a try.

_____

_____

_____

_____

_____

_____

_____

Answer:
Goldilocks went for a walk in the woods. She saw a cottage. It was the cottage of the Three Bears. She saw that the door was open. Goldilocks was curious. She went inside.

The rules for writing paragraphs hold true for every paragraph you will ever write. But when you are writing a report, you will be creating some special kinds of paragraphs that have a few extra rules of their own.

Every good report needs three special kinds of paragraphs: One "introductory" paragraph, several "body" paragraphs, and one "concluding" paragraph. Each paragraph has its own distinct job. And once you understand the duty of each paragraph, it's easy to write paragraphs that perform their functions perfectly.

Let's look at introductory paragraphs first. The word "introduce" literally means "to lead one thing into another." And that pretty much sums up the job of the introductory paragraph. It leads one thing (your reader's attention) into another (your report).

The Job of an Introductory Paragraph

The job of an introductory paragraph is similar to an introduction between two people. For example:

You: "Mom, this is my friend, Ami."

Mom: "Hi, Ami."

Ami: "Hi, Mrs. Nellis."

You: "Ami's a skateboarding expert!"

Mom: "Really? My goodness! Your parents must be worried sick!"

That's the kind of introduction you're probably most familiar with—a way for two people who don't know each other to meet, usually directed by a third person who knows both of them. In a way, that's how an introductory paragraph works in a report. You, the writer, are the third person. You know your audience. You also know your report's subject. In your introductory paragraph, you are going to arrange a meeting between your audience and your subject. It's almost like introducing your friends to your parents.

Now, you probably try to make sure your friends look presentable before you introduce them to your parents, and you probably try to be sure your parents aren't doing or wearing anything too weird when you introduce them to your friends. You probably try to present both of them at their best so they'll make a good impression. You might, as in the example, throw in an interesting detail to add

Criteria for Introductory Paragraphs

An introductory paragraph
- must contain a topic sentence.
- must tell readers what the report is about.
- uses interesting and descriptive words.
- gets the reader's attention and makes him or her want to continue reading.

zest to the introduction and make the two parties want to know more about each other. That's exactly what you are trying to do in the introductory paragraph of your report, too. You want to be sure you present your topic in its best light and make it interesting so your audience will warm up to it and want to know it better.

How to Start Your Introductory Paragraph

There are several ways to start an introductory paragraph so that you get your reader's attention and interest right away. Here are some suggestions:

➤ Pose a problem.
➤ Ask a question.
➤ Use your sense of humor.
➤ Use a noteworthy quotation.
➤ Use dialogue.
➤ Say something out of the ordinary.
➤ Set the scene by describing an interesting situation.

The topic sentences in the following paragraphs are underlined. You will notice that they don't *always* come first in the paragraph.

Inside the cramped submarine, all I could hear was the steady pinging of the sonar and the regular breathing of the pilot and engineer. . . . The pings

speeded up—that meant the wreck was close—and I strained to see beyond the small cone of light that pierced the endless underwater night....

From Ghost Liners, *by Robert D. Ballard and Rick Archbold*

That's an example of setting the scene with an intriguing situation. You can really imagine the tiny quarters of the submarine, and the echoing "ping" getting faster and faster as the writer excitedly peers through the viewport. The spooky, endless darkness of the ocean floor seems to crowd in all around. What will he see? What will happen next? You have to keep reading to find out! That's the way you want your readers to feel.

"Hail, Caesar, those who are about to die salute you."

—The gladiators' greeting to the emperor, A.D. 80–523

The ruins of the Colosseum in Rome still stand—despite many fires, earthquakes and military attacks—as a reminder of the great days of the Roman Empire nearly 2000 years ago. **The huge oval amphitheater, which was completed in A.D. 80, could seat up to 50,000 people. It was used for a variety of spectacular enter-**

tainments, including gladiator contests, chariot races, and even a mock sea battle, for which the whole arena had to be flooded....

From Amazing Structures,
by Michael Pollard

That's an example of starting your introductory paragraph with a quote. It's an interesting quote, bringing to mind images of toga-wearing Roman emperors and sweaty gladiators fighting for their lives. The writer uses descriptive words to get us interested in his topic: the Roman Colosseum, which he depicts as being huge, exciting, and filled with action. We want to continue reading to learn more about this colorful place. The topic sentence in the paragraph is the first sentence of the paragraph that follows the quotation, which sets the scene. (See the Appendix for a selection of quotes you might use to start introductory paragraphs.)

> **Sloths are famous for moving slowly.** One mother sloth "hurrying" to her baby took an hour to travel 15 feet! These strange mammals spend much of their lives hanging upside down in trees in South American rain forests. They rarely come down to the ground. . . .
>
> *From* The Ultimate Book of Bones, *by Jinny Johnson*

This is an example of getting the reader's interest by saying something out of the ordinary. An ordinary mother animal would rush to help her baby in a matter of seconds, but the sloth is extremely slow. And an animal that lives in the treetops and rarely comes down to the ground is different, indeed. The writer is hoping readers may be interested in learning more about these truly out-of-the-ordinary creatures. The topic sentence is exactly where you'd expect it to be: at the beginning of the report.

You can use any of these techniques to make your own reports more interesting. When you are doing your research, take note of how the writers of the materials you read try to catch your interest in their writing. Some will no doubt be more interesting than others. Make note of the opening sentences that get your attention, and use those same techniques in your own writing. But remember, use the same techniques, not the same words. You want to express yourself in your own unique voice.

HANDY TIP:
Even though an introductory paragraph comes at the very beginning of your report, sometimes it's easier to write it after you've finished writing the rest of your report.

A Word About Words

You've been reading a lot about creating interesting sentences and well-organized paragraphs. It's worthwhile to spend a few minutes thinking about the words—especially nouns, verbs, adjectives, and adverbs—that go into creating those sentences and paragraphs. Let's review these common words.

Nouns—words that name things. Proper nouns are the names of specific people, places, and things, and they must be capitalized whenever they are written. Common nouns are words that name general people, places, and things, and they are not capitalized unless they begin a sentence.

COMMON NOUN	PROPER NOUN
building	Taj Mahal
singer	Madonna
championship	World Series
monarch	Queen Elizabeth

When writing reports, use specific nouns whenever possible. Capitalize proper nouns whenever you use them. And if you feel that you're using the same noun too many times, look up the noun in a thesaurus to see if it has a synonym you can use for a little bit of variety. (Some computer word processing programs have a thesaurus built in. Look in your software manual for directions on how to use yours, because each program varies slightly. If you're not using a computer, you can find synonyms in a book like *Roget's Thesaurus*.)

Pronouns—words such as "I, we, you" that can substitute for nouns. If you can substitute one of the pronouns in the first chart on the next page for a word in your sentence and the sentence still makes sense, then use the form of the verb that goes with the pronoun in the table to show "being." For example:

Mammals are warm-blooded animals. They are found all over the world.

Humans are mammals. We are warm-blooded.

Magellan was an explorer. He was a sailor.

Verbs—action words. Actually, verbs do not have to show any really "active" action. Some verbs show "being." Verbs that show being are members of the "to be" family of verbs. They include:

PRESENT TENSE	PAST TENSE
am (I am)	was (I, he, she, it was)
is (he, she, it is)	
are (you—singular and plural; they; we)	were (you—singular and plural; they; we)

The difference between a verb that shows action and one that shows being is demonstrated in the following chart:

VERB SHOWING "ACTION"	VERB SHOWING "BEING"
run ("I run five miles a day.")	am ("I am alive.")
sit ("I sit next to Tim.")	is ("He is my friend.")

In the chart above, all four groups of words in parentheses are complete sentences. Each one contains a subject (a performer of action or of being) and a verb (an expression of action or being).

In your report, you might want to use one kind of sentence that seems to break the rule that says each sentence needs a subject and a verb. This kind of sentence usually expresses a command or a request. Some examples of this kind of sentence are:

Close the door.

Turn the page.

Think about it.

The subject in each of these sentences is understood by the reader. Because the writer is telling the reader to do something, it's as if the word "you" is included in the beginning of each sentence. In fact, the subject of a command or request, if not written out in the sentence, is said to be "you, understood."

The following is an example using a "you, understood" sentence in a report (the "you, understood" sentence is underlined):

> <u>**Pinch your arm or hand and you will feel the hard bones beneath the skin.**</u> **Lots of different bones make up your skeleton, which is the support and framework for your body....**
>
> *From* The Ultimate Book of Bones, *by Jinny Johnson*

One reason you might want to use an opening sentence like this is that it immediately gets the reader involved in the subject of your report. It also makes a good "hook" to interest the reader in learning more about your topic.

Naturally, some verbs are more colorful than others and will make your writing more interesting and colorful, too. The same thesaurus that you used to look up synonyms for nouns will also provide you with synonyms for verbs. For example, searching a thesaurus for synonyms for "run" might turn up the following words: hurry, hasten, rush, dash, flee, speed, race, scramble.

You will notice that each one of those verbs has a slightly different meaning than "run." So even though they all mean pretty much the same thing, you could not use any one of them in any sentence as a substitute for the word "run." It's easy to see that "I run five miles a day," doesn't mean the same thing as "I hurry five miles a day," "I dash five miles a day," or "I flee five miles a day." You have to do a little bit of thinking and use common sense to decide when to substitute a synonym for any given word in your writing.

Let's try substituting verbs in a sample paragraph to see how this works. Say you were writing a report on the sinking of the *Titanic*. Such a report might include sentences like the following:

> **The passengers ran through the hallways of the ship. They ran up the steps, trying to get to the lifeboat deck. Most of them were stopped by gates and guards waving guns, but some got through. Those people ran to the lifeboats . . .**

That's a lot of running around, isn't it? It's not very interesting to read, either. Let's try varying it by using some synonyms that make sense:

> **The passengers hurried through the hallways of the ship. They raced up the steps, trying to get to the lifeboat deck. Most of them were stopped by gates and guards waving guns, but some got through. Those people dashed to the lifeboats . . .**

 That's better. The reader doesn't get tired of seeing the word "ran" over and over again, and the synonyms really help the reader visualize the action more clearly. In addition, the words we chose are all synonyms that make sense in the sentences as substitutes for "ran."

Adjectives and Adverbs—descriptive words. Adjectives describe nouns and other adjectives, and adverbs describe verbs (or other descriptive words). Adjectives often tell how a noun appears to one or more of the senses. Adverbs often answer the question: How or when was an action performed?

Let's try adding some adjectives and adverbs to that paragraph about the *Titanic* and see what results we get. (The adjectives and adverbs in the following paragraph are underlined and labeled.)

The <u>panicky, third-class</u> passengers hurried through the
      adjectives

<u>darkened, narrow</u> hallways of the <u>quickly sinking</u> ship.
adjectives   adverb, adjective

They raced <u>blindly</u> up the steps, trying <u>desperately</u> to
      adverb   adverb

get to the <u>crowded</u> lifeboat deck. Most of them were
      adjective

stopped by <u>locked</u> gates and guards waving guns, but
      adjective

some got through. Those <u>lucky</u> people dashed to the
      adjective

lifeboats.

Notice the way each new addition to the *Titanic* paragraph—different verbs, adjectives, and adverbs—made the paragraph much more interesting. Try these techniques when writing your own paragraphs to create interesting sentences that really grab the reader's attention. The previous samples demonstrate exactly what a good introductory paragraph should do.

When you are finished writing your introductory paragraph, compare it to the following checklist to make certain it contains all the elements an effective introductory paragraph needs.

HANDY TIP: WHEN IT'S NOT SO NICE TO BE NICE

We've been talking about adding zip to your writing by using colorful adjectives and adverbs, specific nouns, and punchy verbs. But there is one word that will make your writing flatter than yesterday's cola: nice.

"Nice" is almost a non-word. It is so overused it has practically no meaning at all. It conveys very little specific information; it doesn't tell how something looks, smells, feels, tastes, or sounds. It just gives a vaguely positive impression. To say a dinner was "nice," or a stuffed animal is "nice," or a birthday party was "nice," is almost worse than saying nothing at all. If at all possible, weed out the word "nice" from your vocabulary. It's just not nice!

Writing Effective Introductory Paragraphs

Does my introductory paragraph:

- ❑ tell readers what my report is about?
- ❑ use interesting and descriptive words?
- ❑ get the reader's attention and make him or her want to continue reading?
- ❑ stick to one topic?
- ❑ have a topic sentence?
- ❑ have supporting sentences that give details and facts about the topic?
- ❑ contain sentences that are organized in a way that makes sense?
- ❑ contain sentences that are complete and written in my own words?

The Body of the Report

You may or may not have written your introductory paragraph when you begin writing the body of your report. As the previous chapter pointed out, sometimes it's easier to write the body of the report first and come up with the introduction last. So don't worry too much if you decide to begin writing the body and then go back and do the introduction later. It's your choice.

Just as your body holds you together, supports your head, and helps you do all the things you need to do every day, the body of a report supports the topic of the report. The body of a report consists of paragraphs that tell about the topic that you introduced in your first paragraph. Using your notes, it shouldn't be hard to create paragraphs that do just that.

HANDY TIP:

Whatever your topic, you should be able to state it in the form of a title for your report, such as "Beavers Are Intelligent" or "UFOs Do Not Exist." Just don't spend too much time in the beginning worrying about a title or a snappy introductory paragraph. It's probably best to dive right into writing the body of your report if you feel more comfortable doing that, and think about the introduction and title later.

Let's say you are writing a report on Dr. Martin Luther King, Jr. Your topic (and title) might be "Dr. Martin Luther King, Jr., Was a Great American." In your introductory paragraph, you would create a topic sentence stating your belief that Dr. Martin Luther King, Jr., was a great American. Then, in the body of your report, you'd use your research notes to create sentences that support that idea. (See the note-taking grid in Chapter 4.) The evidence you'd include in your sentences would be based on the facts, reasons, and details you organized into your note-taking chart (or whichever other kind of notes you took). You would then be able to build those sentences into paragraphs that you could organize in a clear and easy-to-read report. Refer to the outline you created (see Chapter 5) to make sure you include all the information you had listed in outline form. Keep your information in the same order you did in your outline when you begin writing the paragraphs for your rough draft.

Here's one way some evidence from notes could be built into paragraphs for the body of a report on the topic "Dr. Martin Luther King, Jr. (MLK), Was a Great American":

➤ *Great Americans use their intelligence and skills for the good of others. MLK used his skill as a preacher to make speeches that changed people's ideas about African Americans and their rights.* Then you might list a few speeches, giving examples of MLK's intelligence and skill.

➤ *Great Americans put others' needs before their own. They don't always do what's easiest for themselves. MLK often traveled to make speeches and lead marches when he was sick and tired. He missed his family, but he stuck to his goal.* Then you might give a quote that supports this idea, maybe from an actual person (a primary source) who can tell you what you need to know.

➤ *Great Americans have a vision for this country that makes America a better place to live.* Then you might quote from MLK's own writings or speeches to demonstrate his vision, and talk a little bit about how he changed things for the better by trying to make his vision a reality.

Because this is the first draft of your report, it's not really important to make sure you spell every word correctly and use exactly the right punctuation. Right now, you should be most concerned with getting your research out of your notes and onto the page in your own words and in an organized way. (You'll have a chance to "fix" any mistakes in the next stage: revising.)

Of course, if you're just one of those lucky people who is a spelling, grammar, and punctuation whiz, then you may write perfect sentences even in your rough draft stage. There's nothing wrong with that. But some students (and adult writers, too, for that matter) put so much pressure on themselves to create perfect titles and introductory paragraphs that writing becomes a stressful chore for them. It shouldn't be. It actually can be very fun!

In the rough draft stage, you don't have to write neatly, you don't have to dot every "i" and cross every "t." You can spell things incorrectly and even cross things out. The most important thing is to get your words onto the page in an organized form.

> When writing reports for school classes, the first word of the first sentence of each paragraph must be indented. It's customary for the first word to be indented about five spaces from the left margin.

When getting your thoughts out for the body of your report, you do have to be aware of two things: You have to think about what each individual paragraph needs, and what the whole report—which is built out of those individual paragraphs—needs in order to prove your point or fulfill your writing goal.

Each paragraph in the body of your report needs:
➤ to be about only one topic.
➤ to have a topic sentence.
➤ to contain evidence from your research: reasons, facts, quotes, supporting details.
➤ to contain only sentences that are about the topic.
➤ to contain only complete sentences.

➤ to be clear and well organized.
➤ to be arranged in a good order that doesn't jump around.

The body of the entire report must have paragraphs that are:
➤ arranged in an organized manner.
➤ peppered with colorful, descriptive nouns, verbs, and adjectives.
➤ written in your own words, not those of the authors of your research materials.
➤ filled with enough information so that the reader or listener can understand the topic clearly.
➤ interesting.

What the Body of Every Report Needs

Each paragraph in the body of my report contains:

❑ a topic sentence.
❑ complete sentences.
❑ only sentences that are about the topic of that paragraph.
❑ interesting, descriptive nouns, verbs, adjectives, and adverbs.
❑ facts and details that I learned from my research.
❑ sentences that are written in my words, not those of the authors of my research materials.
❑ all the important information that I included in my outline.
❑ a first sentence that is indented.

The Conclusion

You're almost finished with your rough draft! You've created an attention-getting introductory paragraph and well-organized body paragraphs, and you are ready to bring everything to a close. You're ready to create your concluding paragraph.

A concluding paragraph does two things: It lets the reader know that the report is coming to an end, and it helps the reader remember the important points you made in the body of the report by summarizing those points.

To "summarize" means to restate something in a shorter form. Think of it as "making a long story short." You already know how to do this. If you were telling a friend all about a series of events that another friend had told you about, and the school bell was going to ring at any moment, you wouldn't be able to repeat each and every detail your first friend had told you. You would have to give only the most important details. This is what summarizing is all about: retelling a story in a shorter form, but without losing any of the important facts.

For example, your friend Herman was on his way to his baby-sitting job after school when he was hit in the head by a foul ball as he was passing the local Little League field. He was knocked unconscious, and when he awoke, he had lost his memory and now thought he was an opera singer! People passing by heard him singing, badly, on the street corner, and, seeing that he looked dizzy and had a big bump on his head, they called an ambulance. It arrived and took him to a nearby hospital where he was treated and is now resting comfortably after regaining his memory.

How might you summarize this if telling it to another friend in between classes before the bell rings? Maybe try something like this:

"Herman got hit in the head with a baseball and ended up in the hospital! He's okay now, though."

Think of a concluding paragraph as a way of saying "good-bye" to the reader. If you were talking to your friend on the phone, you wouldn't just hang up on him without letting him know you were almost finished with the conversation. You'd give him verbal clues that would let him know the end of the conversation was coming. You might say, "Uh-oh, my dad wants to use the phone. I'll see you later." Or "I have to go, I have homework." And then you'd say "good-bye" and hang up. (If you made a habit of hanging up without any preparation, you probably wouldn't have a friend for long!)

Treat your readers like friends. Let them know you're going to be "hanging up" or ending the report soon by giving them verbal clues, just like you'd do on the phone. There's nothing wrong with using that old, tried-and-true sentence starter for your concluding paragraph: "In conclusion." Because the word "conclusion" means "ending," your readers will know your report is drawing to an end when they read those words.

HANDY TIP:
One good way to give the finishing touch to your concluding paragraph is to end it with a rephrasing of your topic sentence.

Here is an example of a strong concluding paragraph from a nonfiction work. See how the author of this piece lets you know her work is coming to a close.

Since 1879, millions of little glass bulbs have come to life. They have spread a light as bright as sunshine and pushed darkness back into the far corners. The miracle is due to Thomas Edison, the great inventor. He worked hard and long to make the lives of his fellow men happier, brighter, and more abundant in many ways.

From Thomas A. Edison: Young Inventor, *by Sue Guthridge*

The use of the word "since" in the first sentence lets you know that the rest of the sentence will summarize things that have taken place over a span of time—the span of time covered by the beginning and middle portions of the book. The next few sentences repeat information about the topic of the book: that Thomas Edison was an inventor whose major invention, the light bulb, is an important part of life today. The final sentence states the author's opinion (which is supported by the fact that Edison was responsible for many important inventions) that Edison's inventions made life better.

You can write concluding paragraphs that are strong, too. Let's think back to the example of the report on Dr. Martin Luther King, Jr., from Chapter 7. A concluding paragraph for that report might look like this:

Notice topic sentence beginning, "In conclusion . . ."

In conclusion, we can clearly see that the facts about Dr. Martin Luther King, Jr.'s life show us his greatness. Dr. King had great courage when he marched to get bad laws changed. He had great skill as a public speaker when he delivered speeches that we still remember today. He had great vision when he dreamed of a better country for all Americans of every color. And all these things, in my opinion, are what makes Dr. Martin Luther King, Jr., a truly outstanding American.

Notice final sentence is very much like the title and the topic sentence. It brings the report to a close.

Notice sentences that summarize the topics from the paragraphs in the body of the report.

Writing Good Concluding Paragraphs

My concluding paragraph contains:

- ☐ information that lets the reader know that the end of the report is approaching.
- ☐ sentences that summarize the main points made in the body of the report.
- ☐ complete sentences.
- ☐ interesting, descriptive nouns, verbs, adjectives, and adverbs.
- ☐ facts and details that I learned from my research.
- ☐ sentences that are written in my words, not those of the authors of my research materials.
- ☐ a first sentence that is indented.

Revision

Whew! Give yourself a pat on the back! You've almost completed the process of writing your report. It seems like a long time since you began brainstorming your topic, then doing your research, taking your notes, and creating your outline. Now that you've completed your rough draft, it's time to bring your report one step closer to completion. It's time to revise.

For some reason, this stage seems to be the one that gives many students a hard time. "Why revise?" they ask. It's as if they feel they've done so much work that when they've written their rough drafts, their reports should be complete. Sometimes students feel so proud of what they've written in their rough drafts that they can't bear to change it. They think, "It's good enough. Why should I change it?" or "My report is full of facts that are correct. It's not wrong. Why should I fix it?"

Well, you *should* be proud of what you've accomplished so far. Maybe it will help if you think about revision in a different light. Don't think of it as fixing something that's broken. Think of it as developing or improving your ideas.

Haven't you ever created something—a drawing, a sculpture, a playhouse, a model, a science project—and then looked at it later and thought of ways you'd do it differently if you had to do it over again? You might have thought of ways you could make it even better. Revision is like that. It's about making a good thing even better.

Sometimes it's easier to revise your report if you put it down for a day or two once you've finished your rough draft. Don't look at it. Don't think about it. Focus on other interests for a while, and then come

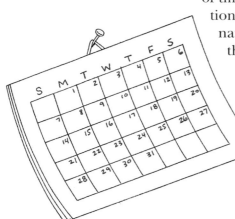

back and reread it with fresh eyes. Read it slowly. Read it out loud to yourself or to a parent, another relative, or a friend. Ask friends or parents to read it to themselves, and then ask for their reaction. Ask them if they understand what you've written or if there's anything that confuses them. Discuss with them what you could include to make your report easier to understand. This is not cheating! Now is the perfect time to use your own opinion and to get the opinion of others you respect, whether they are adults or other students, to improve your finished product. Use this time to your best advantage!

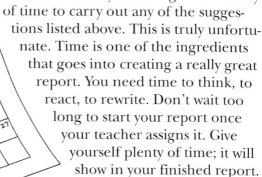

Unfortunately, many students wait until the last minute before their report is due to even begin the process of writing it. Then the due date arrives and they haven't got the luxury of time to carry out any of the suggestions listed above. This is truly unfortunate. Time is one of the ingredients that goes into creating a really great report. You need time to think, to react, to rewrite. Don't wait too long to start your report once your teacher assigns it. Give yourself plenty of time; it will show in your finished report.

How to Revise

Revision is more than just copying your rough draft over neatly. The word "revise" literally means "see again," and when you revise your rough draft, you start by "seeing" it over again. When you look at it this time, you want to see certain things. You need a good introductory paragraph, one that gets your attention and makes you want to continue reading. You want to see that the body of the report makes sense, with sentences and paragraphs that are organized in a way that's easy to understand. You want to see a good concluding paragraph. You want to see dramatic, colorful words that give your writing excitement and life. You want to see words that are spelled and capitalized correctly, and sentences that are complete and grammatical. If you don't see these things, now is the time to include them.

You don't want to see information that seems out of place or that has nothing to do with the topic. You don't want to see paragraphs that jump around, making your ideas hard to follow. You don't want to see the words of some other author copied right out of a research book. And there should not be any misspellings, bad or missing punctuation, or incomplete or ungrammatical sentences. If you do see these things, now is the time to correct them.

But revision isn't just about fixing things that are wrong. Revision is a chance to make your writing express what you want it to express more clearly. Even if you are one of those gifted writers whose first drafts are naturally clear, well organized, and perfectly spelled, capitalized, and punctuated, your report can still benefit from revision. You can use the revision checklists in this chapter to make sure the ideas you expressed in your rough draft say exactly what you want them to say. You can change the vocabulary you used to express yourself more clearly. There is always a better way to write something, and revision is the process of finding that better way.

Tips for Revising

➤ Use dialogue, describe a dramatic situation, or start with a quote about your topic to begin your introductory paragraph and get your reader's attention.

➤ Add details. Don't just write, "I have a dog." Write, "I have a tiny, tan-and-cocoa, blue-eyed mutt named Dingo who looks like a delicious little chocolate-chip cookie with four legs and a tail."

➤ Change some verbs to action verbs. Don't just write, "Houdini came back from Europe to be with his mother." Write, "Houdini raced frantically back from Europe to visit his beloved mother one more time before she died."

➤ Describe what the characters in the report are feeling. Tell what the weather was like if you are writing a report about an event or people that are outside.

➤ Use similes, metaphors, adjectives, adverbs, action verbs, and specific nouns.

➤ And most important: Give yourself enough time to do a thorough job. Start working on your report soon after your teacher assigns it to you. Don't delay.

Revision Checklist

Ask yourself these questions when you are revising your rough draft:

☐ When I read my report over, did it make sense to me?

☐ When I asked my buddies or parents to read it, did it make sense to them?

☐ If it did not make sense to them, what questions did they have?

_____

_____

☐ Did I fix my report so that it answered those questions?

☐ Did I use interesting words?

☐ Did I create an interesting introductory paragraph?

☐ Did I use metaphors and similes to create interest?

☐ Does my report show that I know the difference between facts and opinions?

☐ If I gave my opinion, did I back it up with facts from my research?

☐ Did each paragraph have a topic sentence and several supporting sentences?

☐ Is my report about one main idea?

☐ Did it end suddenly, like I just got tired of writing, or did it include verbal clues that the end was coming, a summary of the main idea, and a final sentence that tied the whole report together?

Editing and Proofreading

You have completed the general revision process by this time. You've made sure your report is well organized, detailed, and contains all the important elements it needs to be a truly complete report. Now it's time to perform two more important parts of the revision process: editing and proofreading.

Editing and proofreading are much more specific than the general revising you learned about in the last chapter. Think of it like this: Writing your report is like building a car. Writing the rough draft is like bolting together the frame and the chassis. Revising the rough draft is like making sure you have everything you need, in the places you need them, to make the car run: You have an engine with all its parts in order, steering and braking mechanisms, wheels, lubrication, and a place for the driver and passengers to sit. Editing and proofreading are more like detailing the completed car, polishing the finish, making sure the chrome isn't rusty and the lights and signals work, and the whole machine is clean, tuned-up, and ready to go.

What Do You Look for When Editing and Proofreading?

It can be difficult to edit your own work. Here are some techniques that can help.

Spelling If you are unsure of the spelling of any word, circle it and look it up in a dictionary.

Punctuation Look at every sentence. Does it begin with a capital letter and end with the proper punctuation—either a period, an exclamation mark, or a question mark?

Look at Your Sentences Are any of them too long? If so, break them up into two sentences, making sure each one is complete and has a subject and a verb. If any are incomplete or too short, fix them by inserting a verb, if necessary, and proper punctuation.

In order to make sure your sentences are written correctly, in standard English and with correct spelling, punctuation, and grammar, it's a good idea to review a few grammar concepts. You have probably already learned about these concepts in class, but let's take another look to help you revise your report.

Some Common Spelling Monsters

Correct spelling is important. If everyone just spelled words the way they felt like spelling them, pretty soon no one would be able to understand what anyone else was writing. It's very important to spell words correctly so your readers understand you.

This is another area of writing where reading will help you. Reading professionally written books, newspapers, magazines, and textbooks will expose you to correct, standard English spelling. The more familiar you become with correct spelling, the easier it will be for you to use it in your own writing. If you want to become a good writer, one of the best things you can do for yourself is become an enthusiastic reader!

It would be impossible to try to present, in one small chapter, the rules for spelling each and every word that you're likely to use in your reports. Every writer seems to have certain "problem" words—

there are just too many to cover. However, there are a few words in the English language that seem to cause problems for just about everybody—even the most experienced writers. We'll talk about those words here.

One of the most commonly misspelled words in the English language is a very tiny word with only three letters. Actually, these same three letters can spell either of two words: its and it's.

"Its" and "it's" are examples of what are called "homophones." ("Homo-" means "same" or "alike," and "-phone" means "sound.") Although these words sound alike when spoken, they look different when written down and they have different meanings, too: "Its" (no apostrophe) is the possessive form of the pronoun "it"; "it's" (with an apostrophe) is a contraction meaning "it is."

If you are in doubt as to which one of these homophones is correct, ask yourself about the meaning of the word in the context of the sentence. For example:

1. The baby bird fell out of its nest.

2. I put it back in, and it's all right now.

In sentence one, the nest belongs to the baby bird. The word "its" in this sentence is possessive, therefore it does not use an apostrophe.

In sentence two, "it's" means "it is." The sentence would make sense if we substituted the words "the baby bird is" for the word "it's." We need to use the word with an apostrophe.

So many people have problems with this little word because most words that show possession use an apostrophe. Think about it. If you were to write about something (say, a video game) that belonged to a person (say, a girl named Niki), you would write: Niki's video game. You would use an apostrophe to show possession.

The same is true for many other possessive nouns: Jon's boat; Mr. Wilson's fence; the neighbor's yard. It's (it is) no wonder that people mix up the two words "it's" and "its." The

best way to prevent having problems with this homophone is to memorize the two forms, their correct spellings, and their uses so you can use them correctly in your own writing.

"It's" is an example of a contraction. To "contract" means to "shorten" or "pull together." We use many contractions in the English language, and they often cause spelling problems. They include:

CONTRACTION	ORIGINAL WORDS
aren't	are not
don't	do not
can't	cannot
haven't	have not
couldn't	could not
I've	I have
he'd, he's	he had (or he would), he is
she'd, she's	she had (or she would), she is
what's	what is
who's	who is

Contractions use apostrophes. Apostrophes are punctuation marks that show where a letter or letters have been removed or left out. The two original words are "pushed together" to make one.

Punctuation

An apostrophe is one type of punctuation mark. The other most commonly used punctuation marks are commas, periods, question marks, and exclamation marks. Each complete sentence you write must end with a period, question mark, or exclamation mark. There are other forms of punctuation, but for your report-writing purposes those will probably be sufficient—at least until you become a really experienced report writer.

A period comes at the end of a sentence that makes a statement. (Just like this sentence.) A question mark is used at the end of a sentence that asks a question. (But you already knew that, didn't you?) And an exclamation mark (!) is used to show excitement. Use exclamation marks sparingly. Let's face it, we all want our reports to be interesting, but very little of the information contained in a well-written school report is so exciting it would be worthy of an exclamation mark.

Just because a group of words. Starts with a capital letter. And ends with a period, that doesn't mean it's a sentence. It could be something called a "sentence fragment," just like the three groups of words at the beginning of this paragraph.

Sentence fragments must often be combined or reworded in order to form proper sentences. Try to fix the sentence fragments from the paragraph above on the lines provided on the next page.

_____

_____

_____

_____

Answer: Just because a group of words starts with a capital letter and ends with a period, that doesn't mean it's a sentence.

First, Let's Agree: Subject-Verb Agreement

We've spoken about making sure sentences are complete and correctly capitalized and punctuated. That's important. But there's another important item to look for when editing the sentences in your report: subject-verb agreement. This means that subjects and verbs in sentences have to agree in number. If one is plural, then the other must be plural; if one is singular, the other must be, too.

You remember that verbs are words that show action or being, and that each sentence must have one. Each sentence must also have a subject: a person, place, or thing that does the action expressed by the verb.

In the short sentence, "Horses run," the subject is "Horses" and the verb is "run." You can see that the subject is plural and the verb is, too. In the sentence, "A boy runs," the subject (boy) is singular, and the verb (runs) is singular. Most short sentences are easy to figure out.

HANDY TIP:
Make sure your report contains complete sentences by checking to see that every sentence contains a subject (a person, place, or thing) that performs the action or "being" expressed by the verb (action word or form of the verb "to be").

However, there are times when the subject of a sentence is separated from the verb by a phrase. In that case, it's sometimes difficult to tell which word is the subject. Because the real subject is far away from the verb, sometimes we think a word in the phrase that is closer to the verb is the subject, when it is not. This can cause a problem if the word in the phrase, which we think at first is the subject, is different in number from the real subject. We might use the wrong form of the verb. For example:

A <u>description</u> of the burglars <u>hangs</u> on the wall of the post office.

This sentence has a phrase between the subject and the verb. The subject and verb are underlined here. The subject of this sentence is not "burglars," it's "description," even though "burglars" is a noun and it is closer to the verb in the sentence. "Description" is singular and "burglars" is plural. Therefore, even though the word "burglars" is closer to the verb, we must make sure to use a verb that is singular—"hangs."

To figure out what the subject of a sentence is, first find the verb and then ask yourself, "Who or what is doing this action?" In the sentence above, if you find the verb—hangs—and then ask yourself "who or what hangs?" it will lead you to see that "a description" hangs, not "the burglars." This differentiation is extremely important because one noun is singular, the other plural.

Try finding the subject in these sample sentences:

1. The theme of the party is "A Walk in the Clouds."

2. The cost of the gifts is more than one thousand dollars.

3. Every one of the boys has a role to play.

4. The design on the notecards is beautiful.

Answers:

1. theme, 2. cost, 3. one, 4. design. Note that all of the subjects are singular.

Make sure you don't get fooled by sentences that have phrases between the subject and the verb.

Another kind of sentence that can be a little tricky is a sentence that starts with the words "here," "there," or "where." These sentences sometimes give writers trouble because the verb usually comes first and is followed by the subject. But the same rules apply: If the verb is plural, the subject must be plural. If the verb is singular, the subject must be singular. For example:

Here are the tickets. (The subject is "tickets," which is plural. Therefore, the verb must be plural—are.)

There is the necklace. (The subject is "necklace," which is singular. Therefore, the verb must be singular—is.)

Where is my soda? (The subject is "soda," which is singular. Therefore the verb must be singular—is.)

There are many more kinds of sentences, words, and phrases that might give you a little trouble when you are trying to make subjects and verbs agree. If you haven't learned about them in class yet, you probably will sometime soon. This book can only mention a few of them and give you some ideas for writing them correctly.

There is one other kind of word that can cause problems when you are trying to make sure your sentences have subjects and verbs that agree. These words are called "indefinite pronouns."

Indefinite Pronouns

You know that a pronoun takes the place of a noun. And you can probably figure out that an indefinite pronoun would be a pronoun that isn't definite, exact, or specific.

Indefinite pronouns are words such as anyone, everyone, no one, some, one, someone, and none. It figures that if a pronoun isn't about a specific person, place, or thing, it might be hard to tell if the pronoun needs to be paired with a singular or a plural verb. The best thing you can do is just remember which indefinite pronouns take singular verbs and which take plural verbs.

Here's a list of indefinite pronouns that tells you which ones are singular and which ones are plural. Use it when you edit your report.

PLURAL INDEFINITE PRONOUNS	SINGULAR INDEFINITE PRONOUNS	INDEFINITE PRONOUNS THAT CAN BE SINGULAR OR PLURAL
several	everybody	all
few	somebody	any
many	everyone	none
both	anyone	some
	each	most
	either	
	neither	
	one	
	someone	
	anybody	

A Capital Idea

You already know that every sentence must begin with a capital letter. But some other words in sentences should also be capitalized: proper nouns and proper adjectives.

Proper Nouns

What's a proper noun? Well, you know that a noun is the name of a person, place, or thing. Dog, chair, building, road, actor, and desert are all nouns. Another name for them is "common nouns," since they do not name specific people, places, or things.

The following is a list of proper nouns that compare to the common nouns above: Benji, Brancusi chair, Empire State Building, Route 66, Leonardo DiCaprio, Mojave Desert.

Other proper nouns include: days of the week; months of the year; names of holidays, like New Year's Day or Independence Day; names of planets, such as Mercury; and names of cities, states, and countries.

When proper nouns appear in a sentence, they must be capitalized, just like the first word of the sentence. "Michael Jordan played basketball in Chicago, Illinois."

Proper Adjectives

In addition to proper nouns, proper adjectives need to be capitalized when they appear in a sentence. Proper adjectives describe people, places, or things. Common adjectives also describe, but in a different way. In the following sentence, there is one common adjective and one proper adjective. Each one is labeled. See if you can figure out what's different about them.

Axel is a <u>wonderful French</u> chef.
common adjective, proper adjective

The word "wonderful" is not capitalized, but "French" is. French refers to the people of a certain nationality. Names of nations are proper nouns, and words that describe languages and nationalities are proper adjectives. Names of languages or nationalities, such as Spanish, are also proper adjectives. So are brand names, such as Nike and Pepsi.

Titles—A Game of Their Own

Capitalizing words in titles is sometimes tricky. When you write the title of your report, capitalize the first word and every important word of the title. How do you know which words are important? Verbs are important. If there are verbs in your title, they most likely convey important information about the subject of your report, and they must be capitalized. This is true even if the verb is as short as "is." Remember that "is" is a form of the verb "to be."

Of course, there are really no unimportant words, but some words are less important than others. These less-important words are called prepositions and articles. Some examples are listed in the box to the right. When they appear in the title, unless they are the first word of a title, do not capitalize them. In the title, "A Walk in the Clouds," capitalize "A" because "A" is the

PREPOSITIONS	ARTICLES
to, from,	a
between, before,	the
of, for,	an
above, below,	
at, on, upon,	
beyond, beneath,	
under, over,	
around, through	

first word. In "A Dollar a Day," the second "a" is not capitalized, but the first one is. You'll often find that books and magazines decide on different ways to capitalize prepositions in titles. The publishers of this book have decided that all of their titles will have capitalized prepositions when they contain four or more letters, while shorter prepositions are not capitalized. For your purposes, it's easier just to remember to make all prepositions lowercase.

You Can Quote Me

There's another kind of sentence that you might use in your report: a quote. A quote is composed of the direct words of another speaker or writer that you use in the body of your report. Quotes are like salt—a little bit gives your writing flavor, but used too liberally, quotes spoil your writing, just as too much salt will spoil the flavor of good food.

If you do decide to use quotes, remember to set them off from the other sentences by using quotation marks. Quotation marks are like two pairs of floating commas that surround the quotation you choose. Always tell who said the words you are quoting, and, if possible, tell where you found them:

> **Dr. Chip Munk, the world's greatest animal expert, declares in his book, *All About Hamsters,* "The golden hamster is the most beautiful of all woodland creatures, and it makes a wonderful pet," and I agree.**

Notice that a comma goes after the last word of the sentence right before the quote begins. There are quotation marks before and after the words of Dr. Chip Munk, and the first word of his quote is capitalized, because it was the beginning of his sentence, even though it appears inside a sentence written by someone else.

However, after Dr. Chip Munk's words, there's a comma, not a period. The quote is followed by another set of quotation marks, and the conclusion of the writer's sentence. The period comes at the end of the writer's sentence containing the quote, not at the end of the quote itself (unless you were finishing your own sentence with the other writer's quote).

Another way to use a quote is to start the sentence with the quote instead of your words. For example:

> **"No matter what some so-called animal experts would have you think, golden hamsters are vicious, destructive rodents," said Dr. Ida No. She is one of the leading opponents of Dr. Chip Munk's campaign to save the golden hamster.**

Notice that the sentence above started with a quotation mark, then the first word of the quote began with a capital letter. There is a comma at the end of Dr. No's quote, a final set of quotation marks, and finally the writer's words, which are followed by a period. The

HANDY TIP:

You will find it easier to proofread your report if you leave spaces between each line of writing. If you write your report in longhand on paper, just skip a line between each line you write. If you write your rough draft using a computer or typewriter, set the line spacing to at least one and a half. Most teachers prefer that you use double-spaced typing. This will give you space to make your corrections. And, when your report is complete and handed in, the double spacing will give your teacher room to write comments about what you've written.

speaker of the quote, Dr. No, was identified. That's the correct way to include quotations in your reports.

Using quotations can spice up your writing. Don't be afraid to use them because you think you won't remember how to punctuate and capitalize them correctly. You can refer to this book as your guide when including quotations in your report.

Another interesting and easy way to see good examples of well-written quotes every day is to read your local newspaper. Make a habit of reading the paper and imitating the way you see quotations handled in the articles you find there.

In fact, reading newspapers and nonfiction books even when you're not assigned to do a report on them is a great way to learn how to write like professional writers. Notice how news reporters, essayists, and authors organize, punctuate, and capitalize their stories, and look at the kinds of sentences they use. All of this can help you when it comes to writing and revising your own reports.

Did You Notice?

In the example showing how to write direct quotations correctly, the name of the book was included in the sample sentence. *All About Hamsters* was the title mentioned, and it was written in italics. When you name books, songs, poems, movies, or other works of art in your writing, you need to set the title of the artwork apart from the rest of your writing. There are several ways to do this.

Use italics to set off titles of books, names of newspapers or magazines, movie titles, long poems, and names of television shows.

Use quotation marks to set off the titles of chapters from books, articles from magazines and newspapers, or episodes of television shows.

For example:

I love the "Rye Bread" episode of *Seinfeld*.

Gone With the Wind is my mother's favorite movie.

I finished reading up to "The Clue in the Staircase" in *Great Mysteries of English*.

You should read *Manor Houses* by Lady Siddoverthere.

I learned that Leonardo DiCaprio is a natural blonde by reading "The Truth About Leo," in *Teens Monthly*. However, my best friend read an article in *Sassyteen* that was called "Leo Dyes His Hair!"

If you write your reports on a computer, follow the instructions in your word-processing program's manual to change regular type to italic type. If you type your report on a typewriter or write it by hand, however, there's no easy way to create italics. The accepted rule in those cases is to draw a solid line under the words that are supposed to be in italics.

Editing Marks

We've been talking a lot about what to look for when you revise your report. But how do you indicate to yourself the changes that you want to make? Or, if you're being a revision "buddy" to someone else, how do you show the writer where to make changes? You can cross out words that don't belong and write in new and better words in the margin or along the edges of a page. But sometimes your rough draft gets hard to read with a lot of corrections scribbled on it.

There are some shorthand symbols that can help you revise your report without having to write too many words on top of what you've already written. These are called "proofreader's marks." There are many, many professional proofreader's marks, but even if you only learn a few of them, they can be useful tools for writing and revising your own or a buddy's work.

Sometimes proofreader's marks are used in combination, depending on what has to be done to make the error correct. See the sample on the next page for an example of how to use proofreader's marks in revising your own or anyone else's work.

Proofreader's Marks

Insert a word, letter, or sentence ∧

Insert a space (#)

Insert quotation marks ⌄⌄

Check spelling ◯ SP

Delete a word, letter, or sentence ℓ

Add a period ⊙

Add a comma ⌄

Start a new paragraph ¶

Make this a capital letter ≡

Make this a lowercase letter /

Close up the space ◡

Egyptians the world's First Sea Lords

We think of the Desert wen we think of Egypt But the egyptions were also good sailers They learned to sail on ther iver Nile which flowed through their desert land. They built ships out of wood and papayas Papyrus grew along the banks of the nile, but the wood was imported from Lebanon. Lebanon is a country near Egypt with has lots of cedar trees. The hulls of the egyptian ships were made by using pegs to attache planks of wood together, the cracks between the planks were cawked with a substance made of mashed-up papyrus reeds mixed with oil. Stuffing this into the cracks made the ship watertight.

The way the ships were built was very smart.

This is what your corrected paragraph would look like once you finished revising it:

Egyptians: the World's First Sea Lords

We think of the desert when we think of Egypt, but the Egyptians were also good sailors. They learned to sail on the river Nile, which flowed through their desert land. They built ships out of wood and papyrus. Papyrus grew along the banks of the Nile, but the wood was imported from Lebanon.

The way the ships were built was very smart. The hulls of the Egyptian ships were made by using pegs to attach planks of wood together. The cracks between the planks were caulked with a substance made of mashed-up papyrus reeds mixed with oil. Stuffing this into the cracks made the ship watertight.

Editing and Proofreading a Report

Ask yourself these questions when you are editing your rough draft:

- ☐ Is each sentence complete and grammatically correct?
- ☐ Do the subjects and verbs in my sentences agree in number?
- ☐ Are all proper nouns and adjectives capitalized?
- ☐ Is the first word of each sentence capitalized?
- ☐ Does each sentence end with the proper punctuation mark (period, question mark, or exclamation mark)?
- ☐ If I quoted a source, did I include the quote inside quotation marks?
- ☐ Did I give credit to the author or speaker of each quote I used?
- ☐ If my report is handwritten, is my writing neat and easy to read?
- ☐ Did I use apostrophes in contractions correctly?
- ☐ Can I substitute more colorful words (adjectives, adverbs, nouns, and verbs) for any of the words in my sentences?

Publishing

At last! You've gone over your report with an eagle eye, correcting all errors and polishing every sentence until it shines. Now you are ready to complete the last step in the writing process: publishing your report.

There are many different ways to publish your writing. Right now, we'll concentrate on traditional, handwritten or typed (or computer-printed) reports on paper. Later in this chapter we'll talk a little bit about some other ways of publishing your reports.

Publishing a Traditional Report

You've reached the point in the writing process when neatness counts. When you've finished the revision process, you will handwrite or type (on a typewriter or computer) your report on sheets of paper. If handwriting, use lined paper, skipping a space between each line of writing, especially if your handwriting is small. After all, your teacher has to read a lot of reports, and after a while, teachers' eyes start to hurt! You want to be sure your teacher can read every word you've taken so much care to write. (Check with your teacher to make sure he or she wants you to skip a space between each line you write.)

You might want to include charts, diagrams, illustrations, or photos in your report. If so, make sure to include them as closely as possible to the spot in the text where you've written about them.

In the last chapter, we looked at paragraphs that had to do with Egyptian shipbuilding. If you were writing a report on that topic, and you like to draw, you might want to draw a picture of an Egyptian ship and label the different parts that your report describes. Or, if the research book where you found your information was illustrated with pictures or photos of Egyptian artifacts, you might want to make a photocopy of the illustration and paste it into your report. But be sure to give credit to the book where you got the illustration, just as you would give credit to a person whose words you quoted. A picture that someone else drew is like a quote that is drawn instead of spoken.

When you do insert charts, diagrams, or illustrations, make sure you label them so your teacher knows why you've inserted them. For example:

Egyptian ship showing the battering ram on the front.

These labels are sometimes called captions. Look through textbooks, newspapers, magazines, and research books such as encyclopedias to get an idea of how to write good captions. You will see them under photos, diagrams, illustrations, and charts. Use them as models for your own writing.

Credit Where Credit Is Due

Footnotes also add an important element to your report. As the name indicates, a footnote is a note that goes at the foot, or bottom, of the page. As you recall, you can include some information from another speaker or author in your report, as long as you make sure to set it off from your own words by using quotation marks and giving the original speaker or author credit. Using footnotes is another way to give credit. In a footnote, you can indicate where you found the quotation you used.

The first quote in your report will be footnote number 1. After you complete writing the quote, write a small number 1, like so:

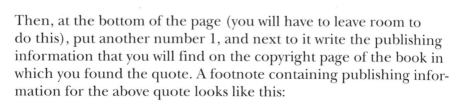

After a while it seemed to Tom that he had been sitting long enough to hatch at least one. He got off the nest with great care. All six eggs were just as they had been.[1]

Then, at the bottom of the page (you will have to leave room to do this), put another number 1, and next to it write the publishing information that you will find on the copyright page of the book in which you found the quote. A footnote containing publishing information for the above quote looks like this:

1. From *Thomas A. Edison: Young Inventor,* by Sue Guthridge, 1947, 1959, 1983, 1986, Aladdin Paperbacks, New York, NY.

Notice that the title of the book used is in italics (or underlined, if you handwrite your report), the author's name is spelled out, and the copyright date, the publisher's name, and the city where the publisher is located are included. This information is all found on the copyright page of every published book, which is usually right inside the front cover, within the first page or two.

Publishing information for newspapers or magazines is usually somewhere in the beginning of the publication (within the first five or ten pages). You may have to search for it.

A footnote containing publishing information for a newspaper looks like this:

1. From "John Glenn's Experiments to Provide Valuable Information," *The Daily Gazette,* November 3, 1998.

Notice that the title of the article from which the information came is in quotation marks, with a comma inside the ending quotation mark; the title of the newspaper or magazine is in italics (again, underlined if you are hand-writing your report); and instead of the city where the newspaper or magazine is published, the issue date of the publication (which you can find on the front cover) is included.

Some publications, usually magazines, also have a volume and an issue number. If they do, you should include that information after the date:

1. From "You Can Stop Beach Erosion," *Our Environment,* June 14, 1998, Volume 3, Issue 6.

If you took your information from the Internet or from a CD-ROM, list the Web site or CD-ROM in your footnote. A Web-site footnote looks like this:

1. From the Nevada Power Company Web site, www.nevadapower.com.

A CD-ROM footnote looks like this:

1. *History Quick.* Jamaica, NY: Punkydoodle Software, Inc. (8806 Parsons Blvd., 11432). IBM and Mac compatible.

Sometimes your teacher will ask you to include a bibliography with your report. A bibliography is similar to footnotes in that it tells where you found the information you used in preparing your report. However, instead of listing the information at the bottom of the page where your quoted information appears, a bibliography lists the research materials all in one place at the end of your report.

When writing your report, you won't necessarily use direct quotes from all of your research materials in the body of your report. Sometimes you just take the information you learned from your research and restate it in your own words. In that case, you wouldn't need to use footnotes, but you would still need to create a bibliography to tell where you got the information on which you based sentences in your report.

Another difference between these two types of citations is that in a footnote, the name of the book, newspaper, or other resource comes first. In a bibliography, the name of the author or editor comes first, as you will see in the example on the next page.

Whether you use footnotes or not, you can still include a bibliography. And sometimes a teacher requires that you include one. So it's good to learn how to prepare one. There are several different ways to write bibliographies; one good way is shown below.

What a Bibliography Looks Like

A bibliography comes at the very end of your report, after the last sentence you have written. You can start it on a new page, or, if you have room at the bottom of the last page of your writing, you can skip a few spaces and begin your bibliography there. Start by titling it "Bibliography."

Under this heading, list the materials you used to prepare your report. If you used a combination of books, maga-

Bibliography

Books
Cavell, Juno. (1980). *Mammals I Have Known*. Henderson, NV: Bo
    Publications.
Messina, Cynthia. (1992). *Be Kind to Animals*. Atlantic City, NJ:
    Pageant Publishing.
Schmidt, Pattie M. (1970). *All About Hamsters*. Hillcrest, NY: High-
    land Avenue Publishers.

Magazines and Newspapers
Animal News. Volume 5, Issue 4. April, 1996. "Don't Have Your
    Pet's Ears Pierced." (Sunnyvale, CA)
Daily Pet Journal. July 4, 1997. "Local Shelter Saves the Day."
    (Las Vegas, NV)

Software and Internet Sites
Animal World. Petaluma, CA. Pawprint Software, Inc. (2345
    S. Cornelius Street). IBM and Mac versions
Mammals R Us. http://www.si.pet/source/start/htm

zines, newspapers, and computer resources (software like CD-ROMs and Internet sites), you might want to divide your bibliography into sections. Whether you break your bibliography into sections or not, list the materials you used in alphabetical order.

If you took your research notes on a grid, writing down the publication information in the separate boxes, you should have no problem transferring that information into your bibliography.

The techniques described above are all used when preparing traditional reports. But what do you do when your teacher has assigned an unusual kind of report?

Different Ways to Present Reports

Your teacher may sometimes assign you to create a report in a format that's very different from the traditional one we've been discussing throughout this book. In this case, you may still be asked to do research, take notes,

Some other written formats you might use to create your report are:

poetry	newspaper stories
journals/diaries	interviews
letters	radio or television scripts
cartoons/comic strips	plays (reader's theater)
brochures	

Some non-written formats you might use include:

models	time lines
graphs	filmstrips
videos	costumes
dolls/puppets	artwork (illustrations, sculptures, etc.)
dioramas	maps

and make yourself an expert on some topic. But instead of having you write about that topic, your teacher may ask you to convey your information in the form of artwork, or a poem, or any number of other formats.

Many of these formats need no explanation. However, there are a few that you might find a little challenging. We'll look at some of the unusual formats here. (Oral reports or presentations are another way to present your research. We'll talk about them in the next chapter.)

Journals

If you were creating a report on the Civil War, one interesting way to present the report might be in the form of a journal. You could pretend to be a student at the time of the Civil War, a farm worker, a soldier, a woman waiting for her husband to return from battle, or a slave fighting to be free.

Remember that a journal is supposed to be a daily record similar to a diary, so write in "day-long" sections, and use descriptive words that would be appropriate for the period you are writing about. If you are writing about the Civil War, your character *wouldn't* say, "I spent the evening watching television." Television hadn't been invented yet!

Using the notes you have collected from your research, you might write an "eyewitness" account of a battle, or tell about the hard times experienced by the families left at home while the soldiers went off to fight.

Cartoons, Comic Strips

Cartoons and comic strips are great ways to recount events in history or tell about a person or civilization. You are probably already very familiar with comic strips and don't need help in figuring out how to illustrate one. If not, check the comic strips in the Sunday edition of your local paper for examples. Remember to leave enough room to write dialogue in word balloons and narration in boxes at the top or bottom of each frame.

Brochures

In some schools students spend a year studying their own state's history and geography. If this is the case in your school, and you are about to do a report on this subject, a good way to present the information is in the form of a travel brochure. One way to get ideas is to ask a local travel agent for some samp brochures and then model yours after them.

These are only a few alternative report formats. The others are not described in depth here because either they are easier to figure out yourself, or they require more instruction than we can cover here. However, you might want to show this list to your teacher and ask for his or her ideas about using some of them. He or she may suggest using a combination of formats—perhaps a written report with a graph or illustrated map. Your teacher might even come up with some other unique ideas that can make presenting research reports a lot more like fun than a headache.

Publishing Your Reports

Ask yourself these questions when you're ready to hand in your report:

❏ Are my lines spaced at least one and a half spaces apart so the report can be read easily?

❏ If this report is handwritten, is my handwriting neat and easy to read?

❏ Are there any peanut-butter-and-jelly stains on the paper? (Reports should have neat handwriting and no stains.)

❏ If there are footnotes, are they formatted correctly and numbered in the right order?

❏ Have I prepared a bibliography to show my research materials?

❏ Are my bibliography entries listed in alphabetical order?

❏ Are my bibliography entries written correctly? (Check the guidelines on page 101.)

Oral Reports

Would you believe that researchers have found that the majority of adults are more afraid of speaking in public than they are of dying? It's true: The thought of giving a speech or making an oral presentation simply petrifies them. Yet in school, students are often required to make oral presentations. And although for some it may not be their favorite school activity, it's still one they manage to get through without too much trouble. (Maybe adults are just not as courageous as young people? Hhhhmmmmm... sounds like a topic for a research report!)

Oral reports don't have to be frightening to people of any age. In fact, they can be fun—especially if your teacher encourages or allows you to get into the spirit of the report, maybe even dressing up "in character" to get your audience's attention. Oral reports can really be enjoyable, both for you and for your audience. If you are a person who enjoys acting, singing, or other forms of performance, then oral reports will probably become your favorites.

How to Prepare an Oral Report

A good oral report should start out in very much the same way as a written report. This means starting at the beginning of the writing process and brainstorming a topic, collecting details, taking notes,

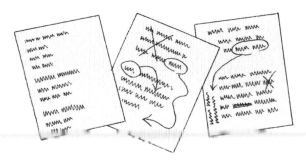

making an outline, creating a rough draft, and including a bibliography.

Did you notice the one step of the writing process that was not listed in the last paragraph? The final step of revising, editing, and proofreading your rough draft is usually not necessary when preparing an oral report, because there is no final draft. Or, it might be more accurate to say that your speech is the final draft, and when you speak, of course, spelling and neatness don't apply. (Unless your teacher wants you to hand in your speech notes after you present your report. In that case, you'll need to prepare a neat and correctly written report as well.)

The one part of your report that you will probably need to polish, making sure all the information is correct and everything is spelled correctly and written neatly, is the bibliography. Even if your teacher does not require you to hand in a copy of your written report when you present your oral report, he or she may want you to show the results of your research in some way, and a bibliography is one way to do that.

There is a form of revising that you definitely need to perform when creating an oral report. You need to practice delivering the report, either to an audience (parents are always good) or to a tape recorder. If you have the kind of parents who always think everything you do is great, they might not be "tough enough" on you. You might want to find someone else to practice in front of—someone who will give you honest, constructive criticism that will help you improve your delivery. On the other hand, if your parents are overly critical, they might get you too discouraged with their well-meaning comments.

Do's and Don'ts of Criticism

• Criticize in a positive way. Don't just say things like: "I don't like..." or "You made a mistake when..." Instead, express your criticism in positive terms by saying things like: "You might want to think about changing..." or, "Can you think of a better way to say...?"

• Always try to blend a positive suggestion with a criticism to make it easier for your partner to correct mistakes. For example: "I really like your topic, but when you speak so quickly I find it hard to keep track of all the facts. Maybe you could try speaking a little more slowly."

• Use the "sandwich" method: When you notice a mistake or have a criticism to make, soften the sting for your partner by making your criticism the "filling" in a sandwich that has "bread" made of compliments. For example:

"I really liked the way you paused between words. It made it easy to understand what you were saying." (compliment)

"One thing you might work on is trying not to giggle so much." (criticism)

"But I wouldn't change the way you pause between words. It's really very good." (compliment)

In that case, you might be better off with a friend or school buddy as a practice audience. You are the best judge of your own situation. But getting some kind of feedback before the official delivery of the report will help, so it's worth trying to find the right audience to practice in front of.

It can be a good idea to ask a school friend to partner with you so you can give each other feedback on your reports, especially if your teacher has assigned oral reports to the entire class. Working together will give each of you the help you need to turn your rough reports into polished gems. But when you and your partner give feedback to each other, remember The Golden Rule: "Do unto others as you would have others do unto you." That means it's okay to offer constructive criticism that will help your partner correct mistakes and make improvements—but do it with kindness, the way you would want your partner to critique you.

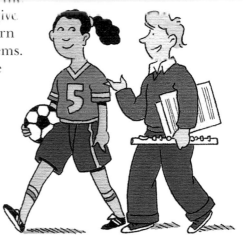

The Delivery

Some things you should try to do when practicing and, ultimately, delivering, your oral report are listed below.

➤ Speak loudly and clearly. Even if you have to slow down until your words sound like they're being spoken too slowly to your own ear, it's probably better than rushing through your speech.

➤ Speak with expression. If you're speaking about an Arctic explorer and you're describing the freezing hardships she endured, make your voice shake like you're shivering. If your topic is something happy or pleasant, smile when you speak about it. Even if people can't see your face, they can "hear" a smile in your voice. But if your topic is tragic, it wouldn't be appropriate to deliver your report with a big smile on your face. Match your expression to your topic and you can't go wrong. (For an example of speaking with expression, watch your local TV news. Those anchor men and women smile when they report on happy stories, and put sadness into their voices and facial expressions when the story is sad. You can do the same when delivering your speeches.)

➤ Make eye contact with your audience. Don't just deliver your speech to the floor or keep your eyes glued to the clock on the wall in the back of the room when you speak. Make believe your head is a camera, and that you are taking movies of the entire class. Start at the door and sweep across the classroom to the windows, s-l-o-w-l-y, stopping to look at the faces of your classmates and teacher as you turn your head a little. If you feel too shy to make eye contact, at least make "chin" contact: As you turn your head, look at some part of the face of a student in each row. The other observers in the audience will think you are making eye contact.

Remember, no one but you knows how badly your knees are knocking. It's true! Even though your knees feel like they're jumping around or ready to collapse, no one can notice them but you, especially if you're wearing long pants. And if your teacher has allowed you to get dressed in a costume

HANDY TIP:

If you get nervous while delivering your speech, some professional speakers recommend imagining your audience sitting in their underwear. It's hard to feel nervous in front of a crowd of people dressed like that.

It might, however, be more practical to practice taking a few deep breaths through your nose, with the tip of your tongue pressed against the spot where your front teeth and your gums meet. Breathe in slowly, and out again slowly, being careful not to make yourself dizzy. Deep breathing exercises are a good way to relax and get your lungs the oxygen they need to help your words come out loud and clear.

to deliver your speech, you can disguise the knocking altogether by making sure your costume covers your legs entirely!

➤ If you are not planning to memorize your report, but are planning to read it from your paper, make sure you do not hold the paper in front of your face. It's tempting to try to hide from the rest of the class, especially if you are a little shy. But putting your paper in front of your face will only make it more difficult for everyone, including your teacher, to hear you. So bite the bullet and put the paper down. Better yet, memorize your report so you don't have to read it from the page. If you do memorize it, it is a good idea to write down key words or topic sentences from your outline onto index cards. Glance briefly at the cards to remind yourself what comes next. If you are nervous, this can prevent you from panicking and forgetting your speech!

➤ Sitting or standing, *be still!* Do not weave or sway back and forth. Try to be conscious of standing still. Use your arms to make gestures, of course, but don't let your body sway back and forth. One way to prevent yourself from swaying is to put your heels together and keep them together while you speak.

➤ Focus on your report. Never mind that the American flag in the corner of the room is blowing in the breeze and touching the bulletin board. Ignore it. Ignore the class pet in its cage on the shelf. Ignore the water dripping from the classroom sink, and the kid in the third row who's biting his nails. Just concentrate on your topic.

➤ Don't become a "Wizard of Ahs." Try to be conscious of the number of times you say "um" and "ah." If you are able to tape record yourself before delivering your speech in front of your class, you might be surprised how many "ums" and "ahs" you hear yourself utter. One way to correct this is to try counting the number of "ums" and "ahs" when you first play the tape back for yourself, then try recording yourself again and again, making a conscious effort to reduce the number of "ums" and "ahs" each time. These are speech habits almost everyone has, and almost no one is aware of them until it's time to give an oral report. These little noises can distract listeners from hearing your message, so it's worth it to try to get rid of them. Fortunately, with a little effort, it can be done.

➤ Don't worry if you make mistakes. No one is perfect. Someone once asked Thomas Edison, the inventor of the lightbulb, if he felt bad about the large number of failures he'd had before his invention was perfected. He had tried 50,000 experiments before his lightbulb was a success. He didn't feel bad about his failures, though. He looked at his mistakes as an opportunity to learn, not as things to feel bad about. So don't worry if your report isn't delivered perfectly. Just try your best, and use the suggestions here to help you.

Delivering an Oral Report

When practicing my oral report, did I:

- ❑ speak loudly enough to be heard?
- ❑ speak clearly enough to be understood?
- ❑ speak slowly to avoid rushing?
- ❑ speak with expression?
- ❑ make eye contact with my audience?
- ❑ refer to my notes only when necessary?
- ❑ hold my notes low, not in front of my face?
- ❑ sit or stand up straight?
- ❑ put my heels together and remember not to sway?
- ❑ focus on my speech, not on what's going on around me?

Summary

Well, there you have it: the rules for creating top-notch reports. By following the suggestions outlined in this book, you should be able to create great reports on any topic. We've covered all the bases, from brainstorming a topic to publishing a flawless written report or delivering a polished oral report. Let's review briefly.

First, (If your teacher does not assign a topic) select a topic.

Next, brainstorm details about the topic to research. Jot the details down on paper in the form of a web or list, or in whatever way suits your learning style.

Use reference materials such as books, magazines, videos, CD-ROMs, the Internet, and so on, to find facts about your topic.

Write notes about your facts on a note-taking grid or by listing them in a web or whatever other way suits your learning style.

Using your facts, create an outline that lists everything you want to include in your report.

Using your outline, write an introductory paragraph, body paragraphs, and a concluding paragraph for your report.

Using the rough draft you have written, polish your report by revising it: edit, proofread, and copy it over again neatly, either by hand, computer, or typewriter, correcting any mistakes as you go.

If you are doing an oral report, practice until you can deliver it smoothly, without relying on your notes too much.

Learning to do research, take notes, and write good reports is a skill set that will serve you well throughout the rest of your life. Whether you plan to go on to college or to go directly into the world of work, learning how to create well-organized, polished reports is something everyone needs to know. It's a skill that makes you stand out. The lessons in this book will help you do that.

Appendix

Quotes and Sayings You Can Use for Inspiration or in Introductory Paragraphs

These quotations—and many others you can find in a variety of books, magazines like *Readers' Digest,* and on Internet sites (type in keyword <quotes> when doing a search)—can be especially useful if you are asked to write a report that gives your opinion. Whatever your opinion is of a subject, you can find a quote to support it. There are many excellent collections of quotations in your local library; those listed here will get you started.

When you can do the common things of life in an uncommon way, you will command the attention of the world.

—anonymous

The above quote might be used to begin a report about an inventor or a performer with a unique talent.

If you can walk, you can dance. If you can talk, you can sing.

—African proverb

The above quote might be used to begin a report about gaining the confidence to try something new, or building on what one already knows to achieve a new goal.

A smile breaks down most barriers.

—anonymous

This quote could begin a report on the importance of being positive in all your dealings with people.

Your time may be limited, but your imagination is not.

—anonymous

This would be a good quote to use in a report about an inventor, an artist, a performer, or another person who is creative.

Actions speak louder than words.

—anonymous

The above quote might be used to begin a report about a person who accomplished a great deal by his or her actions. Or you might use it to begin a report that gives your opinion about whether the quote is true or not. Support your opinion with facts.

The world is so full of a number of things,
I'm sure we should all be as happy as kings.

—Robert Louis Stevenson, Scottish poet

The above quote might be used to begin a report about the importance of appreciating the world around us, or a report about specific features of nature that make us happy, like sunshine, trees, fresh air, clean water, and so on.

A wise person turns stumbling blocks into stepping stones.

—anonymous

This quote might also be used to begin a report about a person who overcame obstacles to achieve success.

To achieve it, you must first believe it.

—*anonymous*

The above quote might be used to begin a report about the importance of setting goals and believing in one's self. It might also be used to begin a report on a historical character who overcame obstacles by believing in herself or himself.

You can't hurt your eyesight looking at the bright side of life.

—*anonymous*

This quote might be used to begin a report on the importance of keeping a positive outlook in life.

No pain, no gain.

—*American proverb*

This quote might be used to begin a report on an athlete or other achiever who made sacrifices but who ultimately achieved success.

Freedom of speech is the most beautiful thing in the world.

—*Diogenes, Greek philosopher*

This quote might be used in a report that gives your opinion. Do you agree with the quote or not? Are there historical or current events in the news that influenced your opinion?

When one door shuts, another opens.

—*proverb*

This quote might begin a report on a personal experience you've had where one opportunity was denied you, but another came your way.

Imagination is more important than knowledge.

—*Albert Einstein*

Do you agree? Use this quote in an opinion report.

The strongest man in the world is he who stands alone.

—*Henrik Ibsen, Norwegian playwright*

This quote might start a report about a historical figure who stood alone against opponents, yet succeeded in reaching his or her goal.

Every human being has a place to fill in the world, and is important, in some respect, whether he chooses to be or not.

—*Nathaniel Hawthorne, American writer*

This quote might begin a report on a historical figure who started life as an unimportant person and rose to play an important role in history.

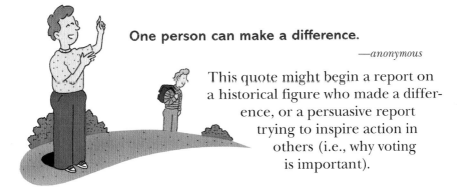

One person can make a difference.

—*anonymous*

This quote might begin a report on a historical figure who made a difference, or a persuasive report trying to inspire action in others (i.e., why voting is important).

A man cannot be comfortable without his own approval.

—*Mark Twain, American writer and humorist*

What do you suppose Mark Twain meant by this quote? This might be a good beginning for a humorous report on what it means to "have your own approval."

Some people count time, others make time count.

—proverb

What do you think this quote means? Can you think of examples of each type of person the quote speaks about?

One kind word can warm three winter months.

—Japanese proverb

What do you think this quote means? It might start an opinion report.

It's always right to vote for the best man, but the chances are that the best man is not running.

—anonymous

This might be a good quote to use in a report on local or national elections that are in the news, or on elections for schoolwide offices.

An integral part of being a star is having the will to win. All the champions have it.

—Betty Cuthbert, Australian Olympic gold-medal sprinter

Shoot for the moon. Even if you miss it, you will land among the stars.

—Les Brown, American journalist

The world stands aside for the person who knows where he is going.

—proverb

These three quotes would be useful in writing about a champion of some kind.

**The trouble with this country is that there are too many
people going about saying, "The trouble with this
country is..."**

—*Will Rogers*

Do you agree or disagree? This might make a funny quote to begin
a report on "The trouble with this country. . ."

Whoever walks with the wise becomes wise.

—*Proverbs 13:20*

What do you think this quote means? This might be a good start for
a report that gives advice on the importance
of choosing friends wisely.

**The miracles of nature are
all around us.**

—*anonymous*

This quote also might start an
opinion report. Or it can be used as a
creative opening for a descriptive report
about a unique animal or plant.

**If there be righteousness in the heart,
there will be beauty in the character.**

**If there be beauty in the character,
there will be harmony in the home.**

**If there be harmony in the home,
there will be order in the nation.**

**If there be order in the nation,
there will be peace in the world.**

—*Confucius, Chinese philosopher*

What do you think of this quote? Do you agree or disagree with
Confucius? Can you give examples?

You are not in charge of the Universe: You are in charge of yourself.

—*Arnold Bennet*

Some people want to change the world; others are more interested in improving themselves. Use this quote to begin an essay comparing and contrasting two historical characters, one who changed the world, one who changed his or her own life. Which kind of person would you rather be?

Success consists of getting up just one more time than you fall.

—*anonymous*

Until you try, you don't know what you can do.

—*Henry James, American novelist*

The two quotes above might be used to begin a report on the importance of making an effort. You might report on an experience you've had that demonstrates the truth of these sayings, or about someone else who succeeded after facing the fear of failure.

Responsibility is the price every man must pay for freedom.

—*Edith Hamilton*

Use this quote to begin a report on men or women who have shouldered responsibility to pay for freedom, such as freedom fighters.

Nonviolence is the first article of my faith.

—*Mahatma Gandhi*

This quote could be used to begin a report on Dr. Martin Luther King., Jr.; or on Gandhi himself, who inspired Dr. King; or to introduce a report on the American Civil Rights movement; or any other examples of people who changed the world by nonviolent means.

Science has promised us truth.... It has never promised us either peace or happiness.

—LeBon

Science has given us many ways to improve and extend our lives, but it has also given us many tools to destroy life, such as more powerful weapons. This is a perfect quote to introduce a report on the benefits and drawbacks of scientific and technological progress.

There are two tragedies in life: one is to lose your heart's desire, the other is to gain it.

George Bernard Shaw

This kind of quote is called a "paradox." It's almost a puzzle. Can you think about what it might mean and write a report on what you think George Bernard Shaw was talking about? Can you give examples of ways that getting one's heart's desire and losing it might both be tragic?

Don't start living tomorrow—tomorrow never arrives. Start working on your dreams and ambitions today.

—anonymous

The bud of a rose is just as beautiful as the full bloom. Appreciate what you have at the moment.

—anonymous

Do you agree or disagree? These quotes could be a good starting point for a report based on your opinion.

Glossary

apostrophe
The superscript sign (') used to indicate the omission of a letter or letters from a word, or to indicate the possessive case.

appendix
A collection of supplementary material, usually found at the end of a book.

bibliography
A list of sources used or considered by an author in preparing a particular work.

brainstorming
The process of trying to get ideas out on paper. The creation of a sudden clever plan or idea.

contraction
A new word made by combining two whole words, leaving out one or more letters in between and replacing the missing letters with an apostrophe (e.g., do not = don't, has not = hasn't).

fact
A statement that can be verified and proven by using the scientific method or other reliable evidence, such as documentation or eye-witness testimony. Facts are necessary to prove a point.

footnote
A numbered note of explanation located at the bottom of a page of text. It refers to a word or phrase in the body of the text that is marked with the same number.

homophone
A word that sounds exactly like another word that has a different meaning. Both words are usually spelled differently, however (e.g., hear, here).

indefinite pronouns
Pronouns that do not refer to a specific person, place, or thing, but to one or more persons, places, or things that are not specified. Indefinite pronouns can be singular or plural in number (e.g., any, all, none).

Internet
An interconnecting system of computer sites that is accessible from a user's personal computer (providing the computer is equipped with a program that allows it to connect to the Internet).

italics
A style of printing type patterned on a Renaissance script with the letters slanting to the right. This is the accepted typeface used for titles of books, shows, and periodicals in printed materials.

metaphor
A figure of speech in which a word or phrase that ordinarily indicates one thing is used to indicate another, making an implicit comparison (e.g., a sea of troubles). Metaphors do not contain the words "like" or "as."

noun
A word that names a person, place, or thing.

opinion
A belief or conclusion held confidently but not necessarily proven by facts or positive knowledge.

plural
A noun that represents more than one person, place, or thing, or a verb that indicates action or being performed by more than one person, place, or thing. Subjects and verbs in sentences must always agree in "number."

punctuation
The use of standard marks and signs in writing and printing to separate words into sentences, clauses, and phrases in order to clarify meaning.

revision
The act or process of improving, changing, and correcting written material. It's part of the writing process.

sentence fragment
A group of words that begins with a capital letter and ends with a period, question mark, or exclamation mark, but does not contain both a subject and a verb. It is not a complete sentence.

sequential outline
A way of organizing data that indicates the order in which events took place: a time line.

simile
A comparison between two objects using the words "like" or "as" (e.g., the baby's cheek was as soft as a rose petal).

singular
One person, place, or thing; or a verb that describes the action or being of a single entity.

synonym
A word having the same or nearly the same meaning as another word or other words (e.g., child, kid, youngster).

topic
The subject of a sentence, essay, paragraph, or report. This is the main thing that is being discussed, described, or explained.

Venn diagram
A diagram composed of two overlapping circles that is often used to compare and contrast information.

verb
A word that shows action or being. It is a necessary part of every sentence.

writing process
A model for writing that includes a number of steps, such as choosing a topic, brainstorming details, collecting data/doing research, writing a first draft, revising the draft to create a final copy, and "publishing" the report by sharing it in written or oral format with an audience.

Index